To Andr...
Lov...
Papa & Nanny
Christmas
2010

TO

_____

FROM

_____

DATE

_____

TRUE HEROES OF SPORTS

Thomas Nelson, Inc. titles may be purchased in bulk for educational, business,
fund-raising, or sales promotional use. For information,
please e-mail SpecialMarkets@ThomasNelson.com.

Unless otherwise noted, all Scripture references are from the
New American Standard Bible® copyright © 1960, 1962, 1963, 1968, 1971, 1972,
1973, 1975, 1977, 1995, by Lockman Foundation. Used by permission.

Project Manager: Mark Gilroy
Images not taken by Tom Dipace are from Getty Images,
Kirby Lee, Hoyt family, IUPUI, Baseball Hall of Fame, Laura Wilkinson, and Bethany Hamilton.
Project Editor: Joshua D. Lease/Aegis Editing
Designed by Thinkpen Design Inc.

ISBN-10: 1-4041-8699-9
ISBN-13: 978-1-4041-8699-6

Printed and bound in the USA

www.thomasnelson.com

09 10 11 12 [MULTI] 6 5 4 3 2

True HEROES of SPORTS

STEVE RIACH

PHOTOGRAPHY BY TOM DIPACE

THOMAS NELSON
Since 1798

NASHVILLE   DALLAS   MEXICO CITY   RIO DE JANEIRO   BEIJING

TABLE OF CONTENTS

INTRODUCTION

What do you think of when you hear the word *hero*?

When I think of the concept of a hero, the word *character* immediately comes to mind.

We look up to our heroes, admire them, even follow them. But how can we do any of these things if our heroes do not possess good character?

I'm not sure that I can accurately define a hero as embraced by the current culture. However, I do know what the parameters for such a classification should be.

A hero is not merely someone who can hit a baseball 400 feet, sink a 40-foot putt, nail a 3-pointer, leap into the end zone, or win a gold medal.

Heroes are much more than that.

True heroes don't leap tall buildings in a single bound—although it sure seems as though they do to some of us. Heroes don't all come in 6-foot 5-inch, 230 pound packages with 4.4 speed and movie star looks. They aren't necessarily media polished and don't always cut rap albums or hang with celebrities.

True heroes are defined by something much more profound.

They are real people who do not live for accolades or big bank accounts. Rather, they live to fulfill their God-given destinies and to use their gifts and talents to leave the world a better place because of their influence.

Heroes are men and women of various shapes, sizes, races, and genders. Many have never finished first, been the most popular, or appeared on the front page. Yet there is something in them that makes us lean forward in our seats or stand up and cheer.

When we watch these heroes, we can clearly see that they possess that special something, that intrinsic quality—even if we're not quite sure just what it really is.

That "it" is the *heart of a champion*. And it is the heart that sets the true heroes apart.

Heroes are people of conviction who always give their best effort, who play by the rules, who never give up, who are consistent in victory and defeat, who help their opponent up, and who live to a higher standard. They epitomize our ideal of a champion; the kind we would like to see on the front of a Wheaties box.

Heroes are passionate. They love to win, but win the right way. They know that their only true edge over an opponent is one they derive from working harder and studying more. They understand that beating the person across from them is not a cause for celebration or a reason to demean, taunt, or trash talk. They know that hitting a walk-off home run, scoring a goal, or sacking the quarterback is what they get paid to do, so they act like they've done it before.

Heroes put the goals of the team above individual achievements. They sacrifice for others. They take younger players under their wings and show them how to succeed at this level. They congratulate competitors, handle pressure with grace, and appreciate their fans.

Something greater steers these men and women: a sense of purpose. They are committed to live, and play, according to a standard they have set for themselves that is higher than the expectations from the outside. They have a clear understanding of what it takes to become a champion and are willing to pay the price to get there—but not at the risk of sacrificing their personal integrity or their families.

True heroes exhibit remarkable courage, defined as knowing the right thing to do and doing it anyway. They see adversity as opportunity. They never let good stand in the way of best. And they know that in the end, an individual is not measured by stopwatches or statistics, but rather by the heart.

In a culture as divided as the one in which we now find ourselves, sports may be the one thing most of us still have in common. While we may argue over who is better (Yankees or Red Sox, Lakers or Celtics, USC or LSU), sports still bring us together.

As we find ourselves needing to share some sense of commonality, certain athletes—who may seem rather insignificant in the greater scheme—have drawn us together and linked us to a simpler past when we first tossed, shot, or kicked a ball in the yard and dreamed of becoming a hero. In those halcyon days, we envisioned being someone who made our families proud, who became a role model for the others, and whose name and reputation were inextricably linked with words like *integrity* and *character*.

The men and women in this book are such heroes. While not perfect, they have dedicated themselves to excellence in their chosen field and in life. In doing so, they have become models—flawed, yes, but endeavoring to serve as examples of something greater. They are people of integrity, faith, and character who demonstrate what we like best about the world of sports.

They remind us why we call some people *heroes*.

ACKNOWLEDGMENTS

This book is the result of years of work and months of research and documentation. As with all projects of this magnitude, I received much help from many caring people. I would like to thank the following:

My wonderful wife and children who give me their constant love and support and often unselfishly sacrificed in order to allow me the necessary quiet time to write.

My assistant, Kristen Martin, who spent hours researching, transcribing, and proficiently handling various tasks to pull this book together.

The Board of Directors of the Heart of a Champion® Foundation for their commitment to seeing sports stories utilized to help shape character in young people all across America.

Mark Gilroy at Thomas Nelson, who believed in this book and was responsible for it becoming a reality.

And Leslie Nunn Reed, a hero among literary agents.

Finally, I want to thank the athletes—the hundreds over the years I have had the privilege to work with on a variety of projects—who recognize that it is not all about them. These courageous, determined, hard-working, gifted men and women have provided so many of us with memorable moments in which we have loudly cheered, or perhaps even booed, and who play for more than the game itself or the rewards it may bring. These true heroes, while admittedly not perfect, live as examples of how to win and lose the right way. I am grateful they have chosen to trust me with their stories; it has been my sincere honor to tell them in various forms of media throughout the years.

CHAPTER 1

BETHANY HAMILTON

Bethany Hamilton started surfing before she could walk. A teen sensation, she seemed assured of a long and successful future as a professional surfer. But how she would approach that career dramatically changed on the morning of October 31, 2003, when a shark attacked her in the waters off Kauai, Hawaii.

Bethany began that morning as she did most others: surfing with her best friend, Alana Blanchard, along with Alana's father, Holt, and brother, Byron. Six other surfers were in the water with them at a spot known to locals as "Tunnels," on Kauai's North Shore.

At about 7:30 a.m. a tiger shark estimated to be 14 feet long swam under Bethany and bit off her left arm, just below the shoulder.

"Nobody saw the shark," said Bethany's older brother, Byron. One surfer later told news reporters he had heard Bethany scream in pain or shock and then yell to warn others. "She yelled, 'Shark! Shark!' At first the people around her thought she was kidding. Then they saw her trying to paddle herself to shore with one arm," he said.

Fellow surfers quickly put her on another board and began paddling her several hundred yards to shore. Holt Blanchard used a surf leash to apply a makeshift tourniquet to stop the bleeding. Doctors later said Blanchard's quick action saved Bethany's life.

They carried Bethany ashore on the surfboard and placed her in a pickup truck to await an ambulance. She remained conscious. The tourniquet, direct pressure on the wound, and the effects of shock reduced the bleeding. An ambulance crew started intravenous fluids as soon as they arrived, then rushed Bethany to a nearby hospital.

"I think the biggest news is that she never cried once," said Noah. "Losing her arm will change a lot for her, but she never cried once. The doctor was amazed."

Throughout the ordeal, Bethany never lost her composure.

"My arm was hanging in the water, and it just came and bit me," she said. "It kind of pulled me back and forth. But I just held on to my board and then it let go. I looked down at the red water. Right away, I knew it was a shark, and I knew my arm was gone. . .I wasn't scared. I didn't think I was going to die or anything."

Bethany's surfboard held the evidence: a 16-inch wide hole was bitten into its left side, extending to within an inch of the board's center.

The weekend prior to the attack, Bethany competed in a National Scholastic Surfing Association contest in Hawaii. She had been runner-up in the national championships at San Clemente, California, earlier in the summer. The home-school student had consistently beaten older girls and women in amateur competitions in the past two years. At just 13 years old, the former Hawaii State champion was ranked number eight in the world and was on her way to a brilliant pro career. She already had gained a number of sponsors, including industry heavyweight Rip Curl.

"We were just trying to recruit her for the world team," said Rainos Hayes, a former pro surfer who now serves as head coach of Hawaii's world team contingent. "She's probably, right now,

> "Losing her arm will change a lot for her, but she never cried once. The doctor was amazed."

the strongest 13-year-old water woman in Hawaii: her strength in big waves, her paddling ability, her water knowledge. She's the best. Her character is such that she will overcome this."

Many wondered just how Bethany would be able to bounce back. Experts said overcoming the emotional and psychological pain of the amputation, particularly one caused by such a traumatic event, would be very difficult—more so for a teenage girl who is bombarded by messages about body image.

But just weeks after the attack, Bethany was back in the water. And, incredibly, on January 10, 2004, just 10 weeks following the attack, she returned to competition.

Stunning onlookers, Bethany placed fifth in her age group in the Open Women Division of the National Scholastic Surfing Association. While she occasionally struggled to push off her board with one hand, Bethany was undeterred.

"It was definitely a good start," she said. "Once I get up on the board, I'm OK. Sometimes it's hard to get there."

She rejected special treatment. "I offered to give her more time (between heats) or put her in a more favorable heat," tournament director Bobbi Lee said. "She refused. She said she wanted to be treated like anybody else."

Despite all she's been through, Bethany has a remarkably positive outlook on her life.

"I look at everything that's happened as part of a plan for my life," she says. "There's no time machine. I can't change it. There's a plan for my life and I'm going to go with it."

Her friend Blanchard remains amazed at her pal's emotional balance. "She stands out not just because of her surfing, but because of the kind of person she is," she said.

CHAPTER 2

ALBERT PUJOLS

He is a sports anomaly—a rare athlete who immediately dominated the game at the professional level and who, as a rookie, performed like a seasoned elite player. He has often appeared as if he is playing on a completely different level from the competition around him.

At the start of 2000, Albert Pujols was a first year professional baseball player. A 20-year-old aspiring baseball star fresh out of junior college, he was toiling away in the minor league at Class A Peoria (IL), hoping to make it big. By the end of 2001, he was a National League (NL) MVP candidate.

Pujols made quite an entrance as a rookie in St. Louis in 2001, hitting .329, with 37 home runs, 130 RBIs, and 112 runs scored in what was one of the most remarkable rookie seasons in baseball history. "He plays like a 30-year-old," manager Tony LaRussa said of his then newfound star. Pujols was unanimously selected as the NL Rookie of the Year and finished fourth in the league's MVP voting. A St. Louis legend was born.

Many around baseball wondered where this Pujols fellow had come from. Not a lot of information on him as a prospect had circulated around the major leagues prior to his first season. Some were asking if his performance were a fluke.

What did he do for an encore? In 2002, he hit .314 with 34 homers, 127 RBIs, and 118 runs scored, and he was second in the league's

The following five seasons put Pujols in an elite category with offensive numbers over the first seven years of a career that only the likes of Ted Williams, Babe Ruth, Lou Gehrig, and Jimmie Foxx had previously achieved.

In 2003, Pujols had one of the greatest individual seasons in Cardinals' history, batting .359 with 43 home runs and 124 RBIs. He won the NL batting title, while also leading the league in runs, hits, doubles, extra base hits, and total bases. His on base percentage was .439, and his slugging percentage was .667. At 23, Albert became the youngest NL batting champion since 1962, and he joined Hall of Famer Rogers Hornsby as the only players in Cardinals' history to record 40-plus homers and 200-plus hits in the same season. He again finished second in the MVP voting and had a 30-game hitting streak.

Prior to the 2004 season, Pujols signed a seven-year, $100 million contract extension with the Cardinals and was moved to first base. Although he battled plantar fasciitis throughout the season, he still hit .331 with 46 home runs and 123 RBIs. He was selected as the MVP of the NL Championship Series as he helped the Cards reach the World Series, where the Boston Red Sox defeated them.

The 2005 season saw Pujols establish career highs in walks and stolen bases, demonstrating his all-around excellence as an offensive threat and the increasing caution opposing pitchers used in

"I consider myself a line drive hitter with power. I just try to put my best swing on the ball every time."

facing him. He finished with a .330 average, 41 home runs, 117 RBIs, 97 walks, and 16 stolen bases—all while persevering through a series of nagging leg injuries. He was named the National League's Most Valuable Player. Through his first five seasons, Albert's 201 career home runs trailed only Ralph Kiner for the most in baseball history in such a span.

In 2006, Pujols began the year with a bang by setting a league record for the most home runs hit in the first month of the season at 14. Through the summer, he was having his greatest season. He was injured in mid-June and placed on the disabled list for the first time in his career. At the time of the injury, he had 25 home runs and 65 RBIs and was on pace to break the single-season records for home runs (held by Barry Bonds with 73) and RBIs (held by Hack Wilson with 191). He finished the season with a .331 batting average, 49 home runs, and 137 RBIs. He was once again an MVP bridesmaid, finishing second in the voting. He became the fastest ever to hit 250 career home runs, was voted to receive his first Gold Glove award for fielding excellence, and completed the season by helping the Cards win the World Series championship.

In 2007, Pujols became the first player in Major League history to hit at least 30 home runs in each of his first seven seasons, and only the third player ever to drive in 100 or more runs in each of his first seven seasons, joining Ted Williams and Joe DiMaggio. While missing time due to injuries, Albert still finished the season with 32 home runs, 100 RBIs, and a .325 average. With that finish, he became the only player in baseball history to start his career with seven consecutive seasons with a .300 batting average, 30 home runs, 100 RBIs, and 99 runs scored.

By the start of the 2008 season, those in baseball all recognized they had been watching a baseball Rembrandt—one of the truly greats in the history of the sport.

"He's rare," said Cardinals hitting instructor Mitchell Page. "You look at that (swing) and you think of names like Ted Williams, Rod Carew, and George Brett—guys with beautiful, pure swings. Swings like his don't happen very often. It's a gift."

"That guy just hits me," said future Hall of Fame pitcher Randy Johnson. "I still haven't found a way to get him out."

"You don't rattle him," said former Cardinals' teammate Jim Edmonds. "He rattles you."

Pujols' reputation as a hitting machine is paralleled only by his reputation around the game as a true gentleman.

So where did this man who seemed to step off the pages of a Chip Hilton book come from? And just how did he become so good?

Prior to the 2001 season, Pujols was largely unheard of throughout baseball circles. No one had him pegged as a particularly hot Major League prospect. The fact that he is a baseball star today is quite remarkable.

Born and raised in Santo Domingo, Dominican Republic, José Alberto Pujols Alcántara was the youngest of 12 children in a family that led a somewhat typical life in the impoverished but baseball-loving country. He did not have the privilege of growing up in a traditional family unit. His father, Bienvenido, was in and out of his life from early on, so his grandmother, America, mostly raised Albert, foreshadowing what was to come. His 10 uncles and aunts seemed more like brothers and sisters to him in what was a close—if dirt-poor— extended family. They lived in a communal setting that resembled a campsite and would not have survived had it not been for government assistance programs.

Despite his meager surroundings, Albert grew up happy and well-adjusted, due in great part to his grandmother. She treated him like her own son and passed along her religious beliefs and code of ethics.

Nicknames: "Prince Albert," "Phat Albert," "The Machine," "El Hombre"

Though Albert rarely saw his father, he knew he wanted to follow in Bienvenido's sporting footsteps. The elder Pujols had been a great pitcher in the Dominican leagues. As a toddler, Albert gained his father's passion for baseball, and by age six, he was playing the game every day on the dusty fields near his home. It was there the dream of one day being a major leaguer was birthed.

At 16, Pujols' father decided to move to the United States and bring Albert with him. Albert and his father settled in Independence, Missouri, just outside Kansas City, where Albert enrolled at Fort Osage High School and quickly became a baseball star. While he may not have had much of a grasp of American culture, the one thing young Albert had always been able to do was hit. He became the most feared hitter in the area, batting .660 with 8 home runs as a senior, and was honored as a two-time All State performer for Fort Osage. Albert then went to Maple Woods Community College in Kansas City, where he hit .461 during his only season at the school.

On February 7, 2007, Pujols became a U.S. citizen, scoring a perfect 100 on his citizenship test.

Even with his potent bat, few Major League clubs showed interest in Pujols. A Colorado Rockies scout filed a favorable report about the young hitter, but the club took no action. The Tampa Bay Rays gave Pujols a tryout, but it went poorly and the team did not draft him. Finally, in the 13th round of the 1999 draft, the Cardinals selected Albert with the 402nd overall pick. Pujols initially turned down a $10,000 bonus offer and opted to play in the amateur Jayhawk League in Kansas. By the end of the summer of 1999, however, the Cardinals increased their bonus offer to $70,000, and Pujols signed.

For the remainder of the '99 season, Pujols played for the single-A Peoria Chiefs of the Midwest League. In 2000, he shot through the ranks of the Cardinals' farm teams, starting with the Potomac Cannons of the class-A Carolina League, then being promoted to the triple-A Memphis Redbirds at the end of the season.

After just his one full season in the minor leagues in 2000, Pujols was invited to spring training in 2001, with the Cardinals deciding to give him exposure to a big league camp in an attempt to better groom him for the future. He played so well in the spring, however, that the team could not break camp without him on the Major League squad. So, at 21, and with just one season of minor league baseball under his belt, Pujols began his Major League career, comparing notes with the likes of Mark McGwire. When the Cardinals were hit with injuries, Pujols broke into the lineup, began smashing line drives, and a star was born.

Pujols was baseball's most lethal hitter for his first seven seasons,

"All I'm thinking about is today," he says. "Going into spring training, you don't try to win the MVP. All you're going to do is help out your team to win. If you can do that, this is the reward that you get after the season."

leading the major leagues in total bases (2,514) and extra-base hits (593); ranking second in home runs (282) and RBIs (861); second in runs scored (847); second in doubles (298); fourth in hits (1,344); and second in batting average (.332). The combination of power and batting average over an extended period already puts him the same category as hitters such as Ruth, Gehrig, DiMaggio, Williams, and Musial. Still, Pujols seems nonplussed over past success and keenly focused on what is next.

"All I'm thinking about is today," he says. "Going into spring training, you don't try to win the MVP. All you're going to do is help out your team to win. If you can do that, this is the reward that you get after the season.

"My goal is to win a World Series. That's it. I don't like to set many goals for myself. Focusing on a single goal relaxes you. . . . Of course I'd take 40 homers, a .330 average, and 100 RBIs, but it can be better. I want to get better every year. I never want to be satisfied."

The intense desire to get better has driven Pujols to work even harder each year. He is committed to squeezing every ounce of production out of his ability. For him, this means hours of preparation and work.

"Preparation is very important," he says. "The pitcher is going to do his job and prepare for you, so you as a hitter must do the same. I always watch videotape of pitchers before the game and even sometimes during.

> "Of course I'd take 40 homers, a .330 average, and 100 RBIs, but it can be better. I want to get better every year. I never want to be satisfied."

"If you finish second, you haven't done enough work. That makes me work even harder. You can't sit in your house thinking, 'Man, I should have won it.' You should have won it? So what? You didn't. Just concentrate on what's ahead."

At times, this single-minded approach has made Albert come across as being too serious.

"I'm a grown man," he says. "People tell me I act like I'm 50 years old. That's the way God made me, and that's the way I grew up. If I want anything, I just work at it harder."

That work ethic is just part of what has made Pujols a success. But it would not have happened without the timely move to the states with his father. Nor could it have happened, Pujols says, without the perspective brought by his wife, Deidre, whom he met in 1998 and married on New Year's Day 2000.

At the start of their relationship, Deidre told Albert that her Christian faith was the foundation for her life. Soon, Albert, who had gone

to church occasionally while growing up in the Dominicans but never gained understanding, decided to follow his wife's lead and become a Christian as well. The change gave him a profound sense of thankfulness and helped him keep perspective in the midst of his great success.

"The Lord gave me this talent and ability to be in this position," Pujols says of his faith. "If it wasn't for Him, I don't think I would have been here today. Everything we have right now comes from the Lord. All the credit for the success I've had with the Cardinals is going to Him, every single at bat.

"I think there are some people who look at me and say, 'Oh man, you are awesome.' They look at me like that, and I say, 'Hey, I'm trying to follow my Lord Jesus.' That's who I'm trying to represent every day I step on the field when I cross the line. I know there are 35,000–45,000 people watching me play, but at the end I'm only playing for the Lord.

"If I go 0–4, I can't bring that home to my kids and my family because God's first, then my family, and my career is the last thing that I worry about. So, when I'm out there and playing, I'm just trying to shine for the Lord no matter what happens that night—if I have a bad game or whatever. I represent the Lord.

"I always say, 'God doesn't need me, but I need Him in my life to survive in this world and overcome temptation.' That's who keeps me humble every time. . . . Whatever we go through, the good times or the bad times, He's always going to be there for us."

Such perspective has also inspired a desire to give back in Pujols. In 2005, Albert and Deidre launched The Pujols Family Foundation to do just that. The foundation is dedicated to "the love, care, and development of people with Down syndrome and their families," as well as helping the poor in the Dominican Republic.

Through the foundation, Albert and Deidre support The Down Syndrome Association of Greater St. Louis in honor of their daughter Isabella, who has the condition. They also support the Niños de Cristo Orphanage in the Dominican, near the place of Albert's birth.

"The Dominican Republic is a poor country," Pujols says, ever aware of his beginnings. "I asked God that if I ever got to play here (America), when I got the money, I wanted to help the country out. That's one of the main things; I want to help the country out."

To do so, Pujols must keep hitting, and keep working—two things that seem to come quite naturally to the 6-foot-3, 225-pound slugger.

"When I walk out of this game 15 years or so from now," Pujols said recently, "I want to be the best player I can be. I want to be remembered as a dedicated worker who never got lazy. I want to be the same Albert Pujols a year from now. I want to be the same person no matter how much success I might have." ■

CHAPTER 3

DAVID ROBINSON

It was a classic example of David versus Goliath. In this case, the David is David Robinson, the magnificent 7-foot-1 center for the San Antonio Spurs. The Goliath is the huge bundle of expectations Robinson faced when he came into the NBA in 1989. No matter what Robinson accomplished over his first nine years in the league, it seemed his Goliath would not go away. What David needed was a rock.

It's not as if Robinson had been a mediocre performer. In fact, he had been nothing short of phenomenal. In his first season, he was named NBA Rookie of the Year and helped the Spurs to one of the biggest single-year turnarounds in pro basketball history. Without him in the 1988–89 season, the Spurs went 21–61. The following season, Robinson's first, they improved to 56–26, won the Midwest Division, and immediately became a title contender and one of the most feared teams in the NBA.

Robinson won a scoring championship in 1994. He was selected as the league's MVP in 1995. He led the league in rebounds in 1991 and in blocked shots in 1992—the same year he was named the NBA's Defensive Player of the Year. In 1996, as part of the NBA's 50th anniversary celebration, Robinson was named one of the 50 greatest players in league history.

He became a fixture on the U.S. Olympic team, headlining efforts in 1988 in Seoul, Korea, 1992 in Barcelona, Spain, and 1996 in Atlanta, Georgia. He was the first male to be selected to three Olympic basketball teams and became the leading scorer and rebounder in U.S. Olympic history.

In San Antonio, his Spurs' teams won an average of 55 games over his first seven seasons and won their division four times.

But until 1999, there was still one thing Robinson had not accomplished, and it became the one thing he was known for. In his eight NBA seasons, David Robinson had not won a championship, and the critics wanted to know why.

The lingering doubt the media drummed up implied that it had something to do with Robinson's heart. They were quick to label him "soft," telling the world he may be a fine player, but he obviously wasn't tough enough to win a title. They compared him to the game's other greats — Jabbar, Russell, Chamberlain, Malone, Olajuwon, West, Bird, Magic, and Jordan — who all won world championships.

> "I can't overstate how important my faith has been to me as an athlete and as a person."

What the media conveniently failed to remember, however, was that Chamberlain and West had each other, along with Elgin Baylor. Jabbar and Magic were also together, joined by James Worthy. Russell had Bob Cousy. Malone had Ralph Sampson. Olajuwon had a bevy of great outside shooters. Bird had Kevin McHale and Robert Parrish. Even Jordan had Scottie Pippen.

Robinson had Greg Anderson and Vinny Del Negro.

Until 1997, that is. That year, the Spurs won the lottery—NBA draft style—and found the missing piece to their championship puzzle. With the first selection in the draft that year, San Antonio selected collegiate Player of the Year, Tim Duncan.

The 7-foot Duncan gave the Spurs twin towers and the opposition twin headaches. He gave the Spurs a player that opponents had to be concerned about and strategize against—both offensively and defensively. No longer could Houston, L.A., Utah, or Portland merely double-team Robinson in the playoffs and force someone else to beat them. Now, in that same situation, Duncan would do just that.

Robinson had his sidekick—his Pippen, his McHale, his Magic.

But an unusual thing happened: Robinson stepped aside and let Duncan become the Spurs go-to-guy. The rookie was the team's Jordan, Bird, or Chamberlain. Robinson willingly played the Pippen, McHale, West role. The mega-star gave up the mega. He relinquished the glamour, the shots, and the celebrity for the good of the team. He played defense, blocked shots, battled toe-to-toe with the league's bullies, and grabbed the offensive garbage. Not only did he do it—and do it well—he did it without complaint.

Just two years earlier he had signed the richest contract in pro sports history. Now he was playing second fiddle? It was like Pavarotti singing second tenor, Hemmingway ghostwriting a first-timer's novel, Bogart getting second billing. It was one of the most remarkable things ever seen in sports. And it paid off.

The Spurs, centering their offense around second-year player Duncan, brought the NBA title to the city of the Alamo in 1999 by defeating the New York Knicks.

Finally, David's Goliath had come down. And it happened because Robinson had become a David in every aspect of character the name possesses. He simply did what he clearly saw as being the right thing to do.

"How many superstars would've done it?" asks Spurs' coach Gregg Popovich. "Not many."

"In today's NBA?" echoed former teammate Sean Elliott. "I'd say none."

"I guess I just figured winning was more important than anything else I could do for the team," Robinson said.

Excuse me? For the *team*?

Most athletes deal with such a move with scowls and vitriolic outbursts. But Robinson responded with a smile and a helping hand. He immediately embraced Duncan.

His approach was exactly what you would hope to see from a true sportsman, which Robinson clearly is. He plunged into a two-year process of self-denial that put the Spurs in position to win the 1999 NBA title.

Robinson devoted himself, on and off the court, to mentoring Duncan and making him the best possible player. He was determined to fit himself in around Duncan's game. In effect, Robinson would pick up Duncan's crumbs, collecting his garbage, and getting the ball every now and then.

The go-to-guy became the go-from-guy.

"It wasn't a painless thing," Elliott said. "David had to make some adjustments. But near the end of the season, I saw it coming together."

For the first time, in 1999, Robinson was asked to play like Bill Russell, the man he had most often been compared with. And the Spurs won the NBA title.

But such humility is not uncommon for Robinson. It's hard to imagine another star not only less infatuated with himself than Robinson, but also less in love with his money.

"I can't overstate how important my faith has been to me as an athlete and as a person," Robinson says. "It's helped me deal with so many things, including matters of ego and pride. . .and given me the ability to just enjoy the victories."

In 1997, Robinson and his wife, Valerie, announced a $5 million gift to establish The Carver Academy at San Antonio's Carver Center, a multicultural and multiethnic community center and arts presenter. It is still believed to be the largest one-time donation by an NBA player, perhaps any athlete. Since then, he has continued to give personally to build the school into a first-class facility for under-privileged children.

"We've tried to meet people's needs in San Antonio on a basic level," Robinson says. "But we wanted to do more. The Carver has had a great impact on this commu-nity for 100 years. And it is a big part of the black community, which meant a lot to us.... We emphasize discipline, life applications, and morality and academics. There will be no toleration of drugs, smoking, alcohol, or lack of respect. This is all part of God's plan for me and my family...I have a heart that wants to serve and bless. That is what I am."

Understating his own accom-plishments and understanding what is most important to him are hall-marks of David Robinson's charac-ter. Nothing better exemplifies that character than selfless acts, such as developing The Carver Academy

or stepping aside in order to take the Spurs to the title.

Goliath is dead. Character lives. The good guy is a winner, the model of a team player, and an extraordinary human being. ■

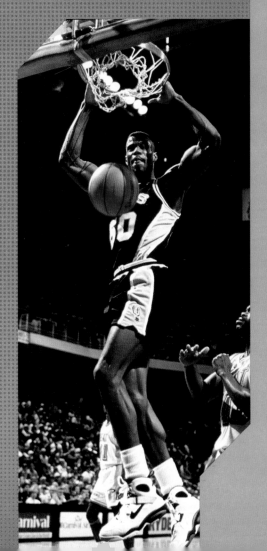

DICK & RICK HOYT

They are the endurance sport family, and they are truly amazing. Dick and Rick Hoyt are a father-and-son team who together compete in just about every marathon race they can find. And if they're not competing in a marathon, they are likely entered in a triathlon: 26.2 miles of running, 112 miles of bicycling, and 2.4 miles of swimming. Together they have become a model of endurance. But more than their amazing achievements of endurance, they are the epitome of a team.

Rick Hoyt can't walk or talk and is confined to a wheelchair. For the past twenty plus years, his father Dick has pushed and pulled his son across the country and over hundreds of finish lines. When Dick runs, he pushes Rick in a wheelchair. When Dick cycles, Rick sits in the seat of his wheelchair, attached to the front of the bike. When Dick swims, he pulls Rick in a small, stabilized boat. On land or water, they carry on.

In 1962, Rick was born with the umbilical cord coiled around his neck, which cut off oxygen to his brain. Doctors told Dick and Rick's mother, Judy, that there was no hope for their son's development. "It's been a story of exclusion ever since he was born," Dick said. "When he was eight months old, the doctors told us we should just put him away—he'd be a vegetable all his life. Well, those doctors are not alive any more, but I would like them to be able to see Rick now."

Convinced Rick was every bit as intelligent as his two younger brothers, the Hoyts were determined to raise him as normally as possible. Local school authorities didn't agree. "Because he couldn't talk, they thought he wouldn't be able to understand, but that wasn't true."

Dick said. So, the parents taught Rick the alphabet, and through the efforts of some Tufts University engineers, equipped Rick with an interactive computer that allowed him to use slight head-movements to highlight letters and spell out words. Within a brief time, Rick was "writing" out his thoughts and communicating clearly.

At last, in 1975, Rick was finally admitted into a public school. Two years later, he told his father he wanted to participate in a five-mile benefit run. Dick agreed to push Rick in his wheelchair. They finished next to last, but felt they had achieved something significant. "Rick told us he just didn't feel handicapped when we were competing," Dick remembers of that night.

And so, "Team Hoyt" was born. Dick and Rick began to compete in more events. The competitions became the most meaningful experiences of Rick's life. "What I mean when I say I feel like I am not handicapped when competing is that I am just like the other athletes," Rick communicates. "Now many athletes will come up to me before the race or triathlon to wish me luck."

Early on, that wasn't the case. "Nobody wanted Rick in a road race," recalls Dick. "Everybody looked at us, nobody talked to us; nobody wanted to have anything to do with us. As time went on, though, they could see he was a person—he has a great sense of humor, for instance. That made a big difference."

After four years of marathons, Team Hoyt tackled triathlons. For this, Dick had to learn to swim. "I sank like a stone at first," he said. With a newly-built bike adapted to carry Rick in front and a boat tied to Dick's waist as he swam, the Hoyts came in second-to-last in a competition held on Father's Day 1985. They have been competing ever since and inspiring those around them and themselves.

"Dad is one of my role models," communicates Rick. "Once he sets out to do something, Dad sticks to it—whatever it is—until it is done. For example, once we decided to really get into triathlons, Dad worked out—up to five hours a day, five times a week, even when he was working."

"Rick is the one who inspires and motivates me," Dick said. "People just need to be educated. Rick is helping many other families coping with disabilities in their struggle to be included."

Rick has continued to inspire. He graduated from high school and moved on to Boston University, where he earned his degree in special education in 1993. While continuing to compete with his father in numerous events, including the prestigious Boston Marathon, they have also climbed mountains together and trekked more than 3,700 miles across America. Rick also worked at the Boston College computer laboratory, where he helped develop a system through which mechanical aids, such as a motorized wheelchair, can be controlled by eye movements when linked to a computer.

Team Hoyt's impact is profound. Together, this father and son have inspired people all across America to see that when people work as one, nothing is impossible. ■

Information on Team Hoyt can be found at www.teamhoyt.com

CHAPTER FIVE

CARSON PALMER

It seems Carson Palmer was born to be a quarterback.

His family members' earliest memories of him as a young boy typically involve his ability to throw things with great speed, accuracy, and distance. As an adolescent, he was what he remains today—big, fast, and smart. Yet his calm demeanor and his ability to learn from his mistakes stood out most to his coaches and teammates in those early days.

In junior high and high school, Palmer stood out among all other quarterbacks. His ability to throw a spiral on target, and with velocity, caught the eye of top college coaches. Recognizing his unique talents, Palmer's parents, Bill and Danna Palmer, decided to give him the best opportunity possible to succeed.

While Carson was in seventh grade, the Palmers hired Bob Johnson to serve as their son's personal quarterback coach. Johnson's son, Rob, was finishing his career as a record-setting quarterback at USC and was on his way to the NFL. Johnson taught Palmer the finer points of quarterbacking, creating a relationship that lasted throughout Carson's college career.

"I usually coach just high school quarterbacks, but Carson had the tools," Bob Johnson says. "He had the work ethic and the drive to be great."

At Rancho Santa Margarita High School in Mission Viejo, California, Palmer started for three seasons at the varsity level. He was the prototypical pro-style quarterback: 6 foot 5 inches, 220 pounds, with a cannon for an arm.

Two state championships later
and Carson Palmer was a highly
coveted college football prospect,
deciding between USC, Notre
Dame, and Colorado.

Choosing USC, he started
quickly, becoming only the second
true freshman ever to start at quarterback for the Trojans. In USC's
pro-style offense, Palmer blos-
somed as a junior and senior. As
a senior, he threw for 3,942 yards
and 33 touchdowns—both school
records—and won the Heisman
Trophy. He left USC as the Pac-10
Conference's all-time leader in
passing yards (11,818), comple-
tions (927), and total offense
(11,621), along with 72 career
touchdown passes.

There was little doubt that
Palmer would be the NFL's
number one draft choice in 2003.
The Cincinnati Bengals had him
signed before the draft, but he
would have to wait for his chance
on the field. Bengals' coach,
Marvin Lewis, felt the best way to
prepare Palmer for success was to

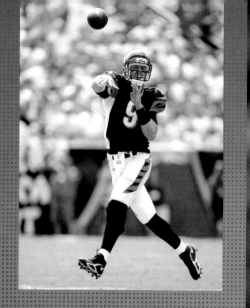

The injury was
called "devastating
and potentially
career-ending" by
doctors.

have him sit and watch starting quarterback Jon Kitna for a full season, to learn the nuances of the game at the pro level.

In 2004, Kitna willingly stepped aside when Lewis named Palmer the starter and became a valuable mentor to the young quarterback.

The plan paid off. In 2005, Palmer threw for 3,836 yards and 32 touchdowns, was selected to the Pro Bowl, and finished near the top of the league's MVP vote while leading the Bengals to their first division title since 1990. A serious knee injury suffered in the playoffs brought a premature end to his—and his team's—season. The injury was called "devastating and potentially career-ending" by doctors.

Palmer showed his grit by promising publicly that he would be back for the Bengals' 2006 season opener. Just eight months following major reconstructive knee surgery, Palmer amazed his coaches, teammates, and doctors by fulfilling his vow. He finished the season by throwing for over 4,000 yards and being selected to his second consecutive Pro Bowl.

Early in 2007, Palmer tossed his 100th career touchdown pass, becoming the fifth fastest player ever to reach the milestone in NFL history. He once again threw for over 4,000 yards to go along with 26 touchdowns.

Palmer remains remarkably humble and unaffected by wealth and fame, say the people closest to him. "He always takes the subject off himself," says his brother Jordan, also an NFL quarterback. "I want to know about the

"Carson realizes he has been given a gift and wants to steward that by honoring God, his parents and his wife."

Bengals, and he starts asking me about what I'm doing."

Palmer handles the fame well because his parents prepared him well for life. It is their support, Carson's increasingly strong Christian faith, and his child-like ability to diffuse pressure by having fun that allowed him to excel.

"Carson realizes he has been given a gift and wants to steward that by honoring God, his parents, and his wife," says the Reverend Denny Bellesi, the pastor who married Carson and his wife Shaelyn.

Yet none of Palmer's success would have been possible without a startling move by his father at a critical time. The summer before his son's junior year in high school, Bill Palmer, a successful financial planner, was offered a job he couldn't pass up in New York.

"I got a great job in New York, and we realized we wanted to live in Connecticut and I would commute," said Bill Palmer. "We took the boys (Carson and his younger

brother Jordan) back there, and they just hated it."

Still, the Palmers went ahead with their plans. They allowed Carson to choose what high school he wanted to attend, and they bought a home in the neighborhood. Palmer met with the football coaches and even went to a football camp with his new team at Boston College.

> "I know I've been extremely fortunate in my life," Palmer said. "I know my family is there for me and they always have been. That's all that matters."

"When I went to pick him up, I hoped he'd be excited about it and gung-ho about the move," Bill Palmer said. "He was miserable. He said, 'Dad, I'm the biggest guy on the team, and they're going to make me an offensive lineman. And the linemen don't even lift. They just sit around and eat candy.'"

Discouraged, Carson determined his dream to play one day at USC was over. "It was horrible," remembers Carson. "Football was so different there. Nobody cared. Plus, I really liked California."

Bill and Danna Palmer knew they could force the issue and simply tell their sons they had to get used to life in the Northeast—or they could do something outlandish and move back to Orange County. Bill couldn't turn down the job in New York; however, so in order to move the family back to California, Bill would have to commute from California to New York every week. He knew it would be grueling, but he also knew it would be worth it. He chose to move his family back to California and log lots of frequent flier miles. They never stayed one night in the Connecticut home and put it up for sale the day after they bought it.

Bill Palmer's weekly travel lasted nearly four years—first from L.A. to New York and then to Boston. The family took two cars to church on Sundays so Bill could leave from there to the airport and head east. He returned on Fridays and often went directly to Carson's football games. He couldn't do much about Wednesday night basketball games, but those were the only events he missed.

"He wanted it badly," Bill Palmer says. "We did what we could to give him the opportunity."

"That's when I realized what a great man my father is," Carson Palmer said. "He sacrificed so much so that Jordan and I wouldn't have to move. He was away from his wife and kids all the time, living in an apartment instead of our house. That wasn't (much of) a marriage. But he did what he felt he had to do. It was tough on him and my mom, but they did it for us. It really was amazing."

Carson Palmer may have indeed been destined to play quarterback, but parents who were determined to do what was best for their son assisted that destiny. "I know I've been extremely fortunate in my life," Palmer said. "I know my family is there for me, and they always have been. That's all that matters." ▢

CHAPTER SIX

RANDY JOHNSON

Randy Johnson can recall his first experience with organized baseball. As a 6-year-old, he attended a Little League tryout in his hometown of Livermore, California.

"I went there by myself because my mom and dad both worked," he recalled. "There I was with a bunch of other kids, feeling like a lost puppy dog. I didn't know where to go, whom to see. I got lost, started crying, and went home."

When his mom returned and saw her upset son, she took him back to the tryouts and got him on a team.

"She knew I wanted to play," Johnson said. "And when I think about it, if she hadn't taken me back, I might not be where I am today."

Where he is today is firmly entrenched as the most dominating pitcher of this era, with Cy Young awards from both leagues. Hitters fear him.

Johnson would never have become so successful without the gentle nudge from his mother all those years ago. Neither would he have dominated the mound without the assistance of pitching great Nolan Ryan, who mentored Johnson in 1993 and helped change him from a "thrower" to a refined pitcher.

One weekend when Johnson's Seattle Mariners team was hosting Ryan's Texas Rangers for a series, Gene Clines, then Seattle's hitting coach, introduced the two men. He asked Ryan if he could help Johnson, who had gone 2–9 with a 5.63 ERA in his previous 11 starts. Ryan allowed Johnson to watch him through a 45-minute workout with pitching coach Tom House in the dimness of the Kingdome. Then the three men talked pitching.

"He couldn't have been better," Johnson said of Ryan. "He was very helpful, and I came away with a lot of confidence. For Nolan, I think it was his way of passing things on. It was very special for me. Just by talking (to Ryan), it helped me realize that pitching is more than going out there and throwing a baseball. It's going out there with a purpose of trying to keep your team in the game as long as you can, even when you don't have your best stuff."

Ryan's lesson to Johnson was simple: Trust your fastball, and don't be afraid to pitch inside.

"I was just trying to help a fellow pitcher, but my role wasn't that large," Ryan said. "Mostly when I'm asked to talk to other pitchers, it's like a five-minute conversation. They come with questions, but they have their own answers. They hear me, but they aren't listening. Randy was totally different. He truly wanted a different point of view."

Johnson's next start was a 3-hit, 10-strikeout masterpiece against Kansas City. A month later, in front of Ryan, he struck out 18 in 8 innings at Texas before taking himself out of the game. He was on his way to becoming one of the most dominant left-handed pitchers in baseball history.

There is one other side to the story of Johnson's rise to greatness, however.

The 6-foot-10-inch lefthander known as "The Big Unit" experienced change in all areas in the early 1990s. From 1992–94, Johnson was hit by a 24-month emotional meteor shower of death, marriage, birth, and spiritual rebirth.

In 1992, Randy's father, Bud, suffered an aortic aneurysm while Randy was flying home to spend Christmas with his parents. By the time Randy made it to the hospital, his father had died. He laid his head on his father's chest, wept, and cried out, "Why'd you have to go now? It's not time."

He was so crushed he told his mother, Carol, "I don't know if I want to pitch anymore. I'm thinking of quitting." Carol advised him to stick with it. Randy eventually agreed.

Searching for meaning, he also became a Christian and drew a cross and the word "DAD" on the palm of his glove. He glanced at the markings whenever he needed strength on the mound.

"God's given me the ability, and I don't want to waste it. That's why I work extremely hard. I don't want to look back and say I wasted the gifts God gave me."

"I became a Christian when my father died," Johnson says of his turnaround. "I had believed in God, but He wasn't part of my daily life. When my dad died, it was hard for me to accept that he was gone. I had a lot of questions; it was very difficult for me to get through it. But God really helped. He gave me strength.

"Yes, changing my mechanics was a key, but that's just a small part of it. My heart got bigger. Determination can take you a long way. After my dad died, I was convinced I could get through anything. I don't use the word *pressure* anymore. That's for what he went through—life or death. I use the word *challenge*. And I'll never again say, 'I can't handle it.' I just dig down deeper."

His marriage and the birth of his daughter, Samantha, affected him deeply. Johnson became a man with a heart.

"A question you have to ask is, 'Do you feel complete?' I feel I am. I've been blessed with four kids, a beautiful wife, and a career that's taken off through God's blessings. Still, I know I'm going to make mistakes, so I spend a lot of time praying. That helps me stay strong in my commitment to Him and to doing what He wants me to do.

"I mean, if you look at it, I was barely a .500 pitcher before my dad died and I got married and had a baby," he exclaims.

"My wife and baby have brought me down to earth. I'm not as selfish as I used to be. Win or lose, I always have them to come home to."

Since the start of the 1993 season, Johnson has recorded Hall of Fame numbers in Seattle, Houston, Arizona, New York, and Arizona again.

"I can look you in the eye and tell you I have never enjoyed playing baseball more than I do now," Johnson says. "Not in Little League, not in high school, not in college. The word *potential* used to hang over me like a cloud. People would say, 'What kind of game are we going to get today?' Now, I'm content. Right now, I'm enjoying every aspect of my life."

Now one of the winningest left-handed pitchers in the history of baseball and a certain Hall of Famer, Johnson understands that while the various seasons of his life have brought both good and bad, everything has been a means to strengthen his faith in God.

"I'm working for Him out there, giving my best effort," Johnson says. "God's given me the ability, and I don't want to waste it. That's why I work extremely hard. I don't want to look back and say I wasted the gifts God gave me." ∎

CHAPTER SEVEN

LAURA WILKINSON

Laura Wilkinson has always liked a good comeback story. "Triumphs over tragedies—I love stories like that," she said after her performance at the 2000 Summer Olympic games in Sydney, Australia, where Wilkinson's tale became one of those stories.

With a gold medal draped around her neck as she stood atop the medal stand for the women's 10-meter platform diving competition, Wilkinson became one of the greatest comeback stories in Olympic history with her improbable victory.

More than 40 points behind after the preliminaries, Wilkinson surged from fifth to first on her third of five dives in the final competition—a reverse 2 ½ somersault, which drew four 9.5s from the judges. Then, on her fourth dive, she locked up the gold by nailing her most difficult dive, an inward 2 ½ somersault in the pike position, which she had botched in the prelims. Her scores were all 8.5s and 9s. In holding off China's Li Na, Wilkinson shocked the diving world by capturing an event that had not been won by the U.S. in 36 years.

But it was how she did it that makes Laura Wilkinson's story so amazing.

That March, just five months before the games, Wilkinson broke the middle three bones in her right foot in a freak training accident: She banged it on a piece of plywood used for indoor training while practicing somersaults for the inward 2 ½. Wilkinson decided to delay surgery—knowing the foot would have to be re-broken and set after the Olympics—and pressed on. At times, she wore a T-shirt bearing the message *PAIN IS WEAKNESS LEAVING THE BODY*. A fused mass of bone on the bottom of her foot made it feel like she constantly walked on a rock.

Wilkinson approached her precarious route to the Olympics with caution, rarely able to practice her actual dives from the platform. She did what she could on crutches for two months. She practiced six hours a day with various types of casts, mounting the platform and visualizing going through her takeoffs and come-outs for every dive on her list. When the casts came off, she wore a protective boot to cushion the climb. She performed most of her dives from a sitting position. The first time she attempted to climb the 33-foot tower following the injury, it took her 10 minutes to get to the top.

Still, Wilkinson was determined not to let the situation sidetrack her dream. Said Wilkinson's coach, Ken Armstrong, "I had never seen that sense of urgency in her."

While her climbs to the platform did not last quite as long in Sydney, she still made them with a protective boot on her foot. So, when Wilkinson reached the top of the platform for her fourth dive of her golden night, knowing she was one good dive away from gold, she slowly removed her boot and tossed it down to the pool deck below, then took a deep breath.

As her name was called, she looked out at those in the stands cheering for her and acknowledged them with a smile, drinking in the moment. She recited a Bible verse to herself, then launched into the same dive that had earlier caused her injury.

"It's the same action that I broke my foot on," she recalled immediately after her performance. "It makes me nervous as I get close to the platform. Plus, I have to stand on the ball of my foot. But I guess when it got right down to it, it didn't matter anymore. I figured I had nothing to lose."

When it was over, Wilkinson had indeed lost nothing and gained much—including perspective to go with a medal and a claim as the world's best diver.

"I knew that I just wanted to dive because I loved it," she said. "I wanted to win a gold medal, but I knew that if I didn't, it wasn't the end of the world.

"I didn't want to live my life thinking, 'What if?' I guess if you find out that if you want something bad enough, then it means enough to you that fear and pain become unimportant."

In 2008, eight years after her remarkable performance in Sydney, Wilkinson made a comeback of a different sort. She decided to postpone retirement for one last shot at representing her country. Looking much like the Wilkinson model of 2000, she won the Olympic trials and promptly announced that the dives she would make at the games in Beijing, China, would be her last as a competitive athlete. While she did not medal at the 2008 games, Wilkinson still made her presence known. She was named captain of the U.S. diving team and was frequently seen mentoring the next generation of American divers. Such actions added to the legacy of the woman who completed her career as one of the most respected and successful divers in U.S. history. ■

CHAPTER EIGHT

MARIANO RIVERA

Mariano Rivera is generally regarded as the finest relief pitcher in the history of Major League Baseball. Through the 2008 season, he had helped the New York Yankees to four World Series titles and had garnered a World Series MVP trophy for his performance in 1999. He has already become the most prolific post season relief pitcher in baseball history—with the Major League record for most saves in the playoffs and World Series—and had climbed to second all-time in saves.

Yet as a man who has found himself in the midst of such intense situations seemingly on a nightly basis, Rivera never looks like a person in the pressure cooker. He is unshakeable on the mound. His expression almost never changes, and he exhibits an unusual calmness.

"Sometimes you can't tell if he's given up six hits in a row or just struck out six guys," said longtime teammate Derek Jeter. "There's no emotion from that guy out there. He just comes in, closes the door, and walks in the dugout."

The record-setting reliever credits two experiences for his ability to handle pressure. The first is his upbringing. The pressure of staring down David Ortiz with the bases loaded in the bottom of the ninth is nothing like the pressure he experienced as a youngster growing up in Panama.

Rivera gained his perspective and his inner strength as a boy, spending hours each day on the fishing boat his father captained. Day after day, the two searched the sea for sardines that they sold at the marketplace to make fish flour.

"Sometimes we'd be out there a whole day and a whole night. Sometimes we don't catch nothing," said Rivera. "It was tough, but we survived."

Survival came because of the efforts of his father, Mariano Sr., who would not quit until he had provided for Mariano and his sister and two brothers. It was a work ethic his son quickly emulated.

"If it wasn't for him," Rivera says of his father, "I don't think I would have this character. His character is strong, and he taught me that way."

Driven by his father's example, Rivera has become the most dominant relief pitcher in post-season history and is regarded as a sure-fire Hall of Famer. But his success serves to further demonstrate how far Rivera has come from his childhood years of extreme poverty in the small Panamanian fishing town of Puerto Caimito.

When Rivera needed a baseball glove as a boy in Panama, he made one—from cardboard. He remembers fondly how much he learned from the days he used that makeshift glove and the days when the fishing nets came up with far too light a load.

"That was the best time ever, the best childhood," he says. "I didn't miss anything. It was fun for me, the greatest thing that ever happened."

Now the slender 6-foot-2 right-hander with the smooth delivery and exceptional cut fastball is a hero back home, much as his father has been to him.

"When we (the Yankees) play, the city just shuts down completely. They're just watching the game," he says. "It's kind of neat."

It is indeed a long way from Panama to New York City, and the spotlight is a bit brighter. It was Rivera's first experience in the Big Apple that provided another source for learning how to handle pressure and set the course for his future.

In 1995, he was a 25-year-old rookie who was anything but

calm. He was the Yankees' set-up man for then closer John Wetteland and was a bit overwhelmed by life in the big leagues and life in the Big Apple.

Rivera is quick to point out the influence his predecessor had on his life. He observed as Wetteland became the game's premier closer with New York in the mid-nineties. He watched Wetteland handle the attention and pressure of the media and how he dealt with heart-breaking failures and great successes—including the 1996 World Series MVP award. Rivera watched Wetteland's demeanor and studied his character. He liked what he saw.

"John was like a teacher for me," Rivera says. "He was the first guy that I met who was a Christian. We talked a lot about the Bible and about the game. I was a rookie (in 1995), and then in my second year in the big leagues, here I am, talking with the best closer. He came to be more of my friend, my family. That's why I say that year is special. That year just kind of opened up the way for me to go through."

Wetteland's example gave Rivera a model for how to approach his profession and his life.

"The world gives you fame, gives you a power; but the Lord gives you peace, and love," says Rivera. "It's a love that nobody else can give you. Not even the world can give you that."

That peace was never more evident than at the conclusion of the 2001 World Series. Rivera was on the mound as the Arizona Diamondbacks rallied in the bottom of the 9th inning to win Game Seven and take the championship. It was the first time Rivera had either failed to save or lost a Series game. Yet, much like Wetteland, he was mostly unfazed.

"Those are the major things as a pitcher you have to confront— blowing saves," Rivera said. "And when I do that, I have to forget everything. I even have to forget when I do (well), because it has passed already. I have to look forward and move on. And when I do that, everything else takes care of itself.

"God has helped me a lot to carry on in my life. Yes, this is what I love, but this will pass. This will pass and everything will be fine," he said of that moment. "You know, you win, you lose. When I lost the World Series, that was tough for me, but He gave me the peace. He gave me the strength to move on. And nobody will give me that. No man will give me that strength—will give me that peace, that love. He gave me that. That's why I move on.

"The Lord gives you peace and love; and it's a love that nobody else can give you." ■

CHAPTER NINE

JACKIE ROBINSON

On April 15, 1947, Jackie Robinson crossed the white line.

He crossed the white chalk line that outlined the baseball diamond and the line of color separation that kept America's game in bondage to bigotry.

But Robinson didn't just break baseball's color barrier by becoming the first black major leaguer of the century. He also set into motion the most sweeping social changes in the nation's history. For the first time, America had a black hero at the very center of the country's consciousness. More than his talent, it was Robinson's resolve and extraordinary self-control that made it possible.

Brooklyn Dodgers' president, Branch Rickey, signed Robinson with the intent of seeing him as the torch-bearer for integration in baseball. Rickey prepared his young player for the barrage he would have to endure in 1947, knowing the first black player would have to survive all manner of provocation—emotional and physical. In Robinson, he saw a man with the fortitude to withstand even the harshest of opposition.

Robinson endured the most vicious treatment any athlete has ever faced. He was the target of racial epithets and flying cleats, of hate letters and death threats, of pitchers throwing at his head and legs, and catchers spitting on his shoes. In the midst of this chaos, there was a circus-like quality to Dodgers' games, with Robinson on display. Large crowds, including many African-Americans, cheered his pop-ups and ground-outs. The daily papers singled him out by use of racial monikers rather than by name.

"More eyes were on Jackie than on any rookie who ever played," recalls Rex Barney, a Brooklyn reliever that year.

As the first days unfolded, the pressure increased. Police investigated letters that had threatened Robinson's life.

"He turned them over to me," announced Rickey. "Two of the notes were so vicious that I felt they should be investigated."

The pressure also involved Robinson's lodging when the Dodgers arrived in Philly. The players usually stayed at the Benjamin Franklin Hotel, but when they arrived there, the hotel manager turned them away, telling the team's traveling secretary, Harold Parrott, "Don't bring your team back here while you have any Niggers with you!" The Dodgers ended up staying at the Warrick. Parrott later wrote that Robinson looked pained over the incident, "knowing we were pariahs because of him."

> During his 10 seasons, the Dodgers won six pennants and a world championship. He was the team's catalyst, a second baseman who found numerous ways to beat the opponent. He was daring and exuded a competitive fire.

In the midst of such turmoil, Robinson soldiered on. "I'm just going along playing the best ball I know and doing my best to make good," he said. "Boy, it's rugged."

Robinson eventually won over most observers. He was named National League Rookie of the Year in 1947 and then went on to be voted the league's Most Valuable Player two years later. During his 10 seasons, the Dodgers won six pennants and a world championship. He was the team's catalyst, a second baseman who found numerous ways to beat the opponent. He was daring and exuded a competitive fire. He won a batting title, drove in 100 runs in a season, stole home 19 times, and hardly ever struck out.

Robinson's middle infield partner, shortstop Harold "Pee Wee" Reese, when remembering his friend's display of courage said, "I don't know any other ballplayer who could have done what he did—to be able to hit with everybody yelling at him. He had to block all that out. To do what he did has got to be the most tremendous thing I've ever seen in all of sports."

"I'm not concerned with you liking or disliking me," Robinson said. "All I ask is that you respect me as a human being."

Respect came from the entire nation, as did admiration. Robinson had not only carried the future of the game on his back, but also the future of an entire people. The sense of burden was not lost on him, yet he never showed it publicly, choosing instead to constantly demonstrate self-control. In so doing, he gave to baseball and his country more than he had ever dreamed possible. ■

CHAPTER TEN

ALLYSON FELIX

She is a young woman going somewhere fast.

She is Allyson Felix, one of the world's great female sprinters. She has lived with the constant comparisons to the greats of eras past while running past every current opponent in the world on her way to virtual dominance of her generation.

"Allyson didn't run track until basically ninth grade," said her father, Paul Felix. "That was the first time she put on track shoes."

Recalls Allyson's mother, Marlean: "She tried out for the track team, and the coach thought his stopwatch was broken, and so he had to go back and have her try again. And I think she was running in these big basketball shoes, but yet he pointed out that she was just so quick."

When Allyson was in the ninth grade, she made it to the California high school state finals. In the tenth grade, she won the state title in the 100 meters. And by twelfth grade, she started running with some of the world's elite athletes.

"She's 17 and she's running against some 25-year-olds," said Marlean. "For track and field, 24, 25 seems to be the prime for women, and here she was beating them."

At 18 years old, Allyson stunned the track and field world by running to a silver medal in the 200 meters at the 2004 Olympics in Athens. She also broke the world junior record in the event. A year later, at 19, she won the world championship. It was clear that the teen from California had arrived.

"When they put that wreath on her head and when they hung that medal around her neck, it all came together," said her mother. "And I

have flashes of her on the track —
all that she had gone through to
reach this point at such a tender
age, and the emotions just over-
took me."

"I think just receiving my
medal, I just felt really proud,"
said Allyson. "I think when I
initially had finished the race, I
was disappointed. But through my
family's help, they helped me put
everything into perspective, and I
think at that time I was able to see
what I had accomplished and see
the amount of time it took me."

She would experience that
sense of momentary disappointment again, but not often. Her
world championship run lasted
through 2007, and in 2008, she re-
peated as the silver medalist in the
200 meters at the Olympic Games
in Beijing, China. While the gold
eluded her grasp once again, Allyson remained gracious and humble
in her accomplishment.

"We've tried to train her not
to bring the attention to herself,"
says her father. "So very rarely

would she show emotions when
she wins a race. She'll never be
the kind of individual who pumps
up her hand with number one or
anything like that."

"Everyone is always watching
you and everything that you do,"
Allyson says. "So I feel like that's
your best opportunity to really
show what you're about."

A support system is critical for
most athletes. Much of Allyson's
humility comes through the support of her own family. Her father
has been a mentor and has helped
Allyson set her life on a solid
foundation. Her brother Wes has
been part training partner and part
cheerleader.

"They really have a special
relationship," says her father of
Allyson's close bond with her
brother. "They live together in
downtown L.A., and he's big
brother and spoils her and watch-
es over her and takes care of her."

Allyson concurs. "My relationship with my brother is a special
one and a really great one."

"I always want to be there for her, and I think that's the best way I can be an older brother," says Wes.

The world watched as the Felix family surrounded a disappointed Allyson following her second place finish in the 200-meter run in Beijing. They lifted her spirits by reminding her of what she had just accomplished, and helped her gain perspective.

As part of that perspective, Allyson decided in the summer of 2008 to take part in a new drug testing program. Tired of the proverbial black cloud performance enhancing drugs have cast over the U.S. Track & Field program, Felix fought her own public war. She volunteered to submit to a significant number of random tests, which were both uncomfortable and inconvenient. Yet, Allyson knew that her actions could help bring credibility back to the sport and allow her to demonstrate the values she has based her life upon.

"She's just trying to be the best that God would want her to be."

"I just felt like whatever I can do to prove I'm clean, no matter what time I have to wake up or where I have to drive, I'm willing," Felix told the *Los Angeles Times*. "I feel more responsible myself to be a role model for younger kids. . . . That's important to me.

"I'm trying to make a name for myself, and I hope that after I run, I hope that people can distinguish the character and the way I present myself—so that's what I am really striving for."

Her parents were understandably proud of their daughter's stance.

"She's just trying to be the best that God would want her to be," said Marlean.

"He (God) is watching over me," Allyson agrees. "And I'm just praying for His will to be done in my life." ■

CHAPTER ELEVEN

CHRIS PAUL

Chris Paul is one of the game's most exciting players and the epitome of the new breed of point guard.

With his ability to create shots and penetrate, he is nearly unstoppable on offense. He is fearless taking the ball inside against the big men, can hit a jumper from almost anywhere on the court, and is consistently in double figures in assists.

Opposing defenses know that when he is on, they are in for a long night.

"I truly love my job," Paul says. "I get to wake up every morning and say, 'I play basketball for my living.'

"When I'm on the court, it's all about the task at hand, and this is my battleground."

"He's a buzz saw on the court, and whenever he steps on the court, it's business," says Charles Paul, Chris's father. "He wants to win."

"When I'm playing, I'm in a totally different world," says Chris. "On the court, nothing else in the world matters except for beating the other team and beating the other guy in front of me."

"He always had big dreams," says Chris's brother C.J. "He'd never let anybody tell him that he couldn't do something. Just like when he came (into the) NBA, some people said he was too small then. I mean, he's proved so many people wrong."

"I've just always been extremely, extremely competitive," says Chris. "So when I walk onto the court, it can be the tallest man in the

world, could be the shortest—
I'm gonna play the same way,
and that's just the way I've
always been."

While he has become one of
the elite players in the game—a
star who single-handedly
changes the game and forces
opposing teams to game plan to
stop him—Chris Paul is at heart
a team player.

"Teamwork is everything—
especially in basketball.
Everything starts and ends with
the point guard, offensively and
defensively," says Chris.

"I start off the game the same
way just about every time, and I
get my teammates involved. And I
just score when I have to."

"When he has to" is more often
than opponents would like, and
often comes in a circus variety—
an array of highlight reel shots has
made him a fan favorite all over
the world. Yet Paul believes it is
better to give than to receive.

"My favorite moment in a
game is when I make a nice move
and give it to one of my teammates and they score," says Chris.
"When I see the excitement on
their face, it makes me feel good
to know that they're happy (and)
makes me happy."

That spirit of teamwork began
in Chris's childhood. His family
developed a support network and
protective system that still continues today.

"I'm lucky in that I have a
family that's always been there for
me," Chris says. "Everyone who
knows me may know my parents
before they know me.

"My parents love basketball,
they love sports, and I think that's
where we bond even more.

"I know when my parents are
at my games, they're not just there
because I'm playing. They're
there because they're basketball
junkies. They want to see the
game. They want to know what's
happening. And they're there to
support me."

"I thank God every day (for)
where He's got all of us, my whole

family at this time in our life," says Charles. "Just watching him on the basketball court is just an extension of God's love."

Through his family, Chris learned how to succeed on and off the court and developed a foundation of faith—a faith that today is his source, keeps him grounded, and drives him.

"I think when you have God in your life, you feel like there's nobody that can touch you," says Chris. "To have that rock, that constant; there's no one—when you have that rock as Jesus Christ—that can take that away from you.

"It's truly a privilege to be in the NBA. And I understand that it's nothing that I've done; it's all by God's grace and Him giving me this opportunity to use basketball as a platform.

"When you know God as that rock and that foundation, then you always have somebody to call on. . . always." ■

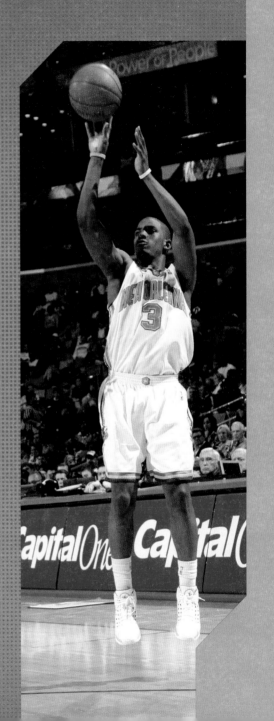

CHAPTER TWELVE

MARK RICHT

In the 1980s, Mark Richt was a backup quarterback at the University of Miami, Florida. Today, he is one of the hottest head coaches in college football at the University of Georgia.

In his first seven seasons at Georgia, he won two Southeastern Conference championships, three SEC Eastern Division titles, and posted a 72–19 record. He was named SEC Coach of the Year in both 2002 and 2005. And his 2007 team finished 11–2 and ranked number two in the country. He is one of only nine head coaches in Division I-A history to record sixty or more wins in his first six seasons and seventy or more wins in his first seven seasons.

But even Richt could not have seen this coming twenty-five years ago.

At Miami, Richt was living fast and playing little, stuck behind a group of future NFL quarterbacks that included Hall of Famer Jim Kelly. But Richt was a great student of the game with a very creative mind. When his playing days at Miami finished, Richt was offered a spot as a graduate assistant at Florida State University. The position not only gave him the opportunity to learn under Bobby Bowden—perhaps, then, the most creative offensive mind in the game—but it also provided grounding for his future.

After a brief stint as a graduate assistant, Richt spent fourteen seasons as quarterback's coach at FSU—the last seven also as offensive coordinator of one of the most prolific offensive attacks in college football history. The Seminoles won two national championships during that span.

Richt sent five Seminole quarterbacks to the NFL while pupils
Charlie Ward and Chris Weinke both received college football's most
hallowed honor: the Heisman Trophy.

But the offensive mastermind desires to do more than win games—he
wants to build model citizens out of his players and leave footprints in
his path others can follow for years to come.

He is a man whose philosophy is shaped by a verse from the Bible:
"Whatever you do, do your work heartily, as for the Lord
rather than for men" (Colossians 3:23).

Such perspective was first realized when his
on-field mentor, Bowden, provided his most valuable off-field wisdom in sharing his faith with Richt.
The pupil chose to follow the advice of the mentor
and became a Christian.

"If your motives aren't pure and all you're trying
to do is serve yourself, everything you get usually
ends up being pretty empty," Richt said. "You get
off on the wrong track.

"I hope that I'm honoring (Christ) by what I do, not
just by what I say. Modeling how a father should treat his
children, how a husband should treat his wife. How a person
should treat another person, how a person in authority should develop
who they're in authority over."

Richt has become a model for Athens, Georgia, being faithful
by how he leads men and how he leads his family. He and his wife,
Katharyn, have four children—the two youngest of which were
adopted from an orphanage in the Ukraine. Son Zack was left in a
dresser drawer in an abandoned apartment. Daughter Anya's natural
parents gave her to the state because they felt they could not take care

"He sets a great
example for his
players and for
other men."

of her.

A family in Richt's Sunday school class at the church they attended while Mark was at Florida State, first talked to the couple about the possibility of adopting.

"The discussion came up about who should be responsible for taking care of the orphans, the widows, the poor—some of the problems in society," Richt told the Baptist Press. "We're really called as a church to help those situations, and that's where we recognized we are the church and what are we doing to help in these areas. All that together prompted us to seriously consider (adopting)."

Richt has made his family the focus.

"They're the only thing in the long run that's going to make a hill of beans," Richt said. "There are a lot of lives that I hope to influence in a positive way at my job, certainly. But if I have a lot of victories there and fail with my family, it would be a sad time."

Since he first set foot on campus in 2002, Richt has made an effort to affect people at the school and in the community.

"He sets a great example for his players and for other men," said Claude McBride, chaplain emeritus of Georgia football.

"I'm hoping that it honors God—that it will help someone," Richt said. "Maybe it encourages people to do things right in their business dealings, at their jobs, or whatever they do.

"I've been very blessed as a professional to be on teams that have succeeded, but I'm no different today because of the national championships," he said. "My relationships with (the players) as people are much more important."

Richt has kept that "people first" philosophy.

"When I go to work, I have responsibilities to Coach Dooley (Georgia Athletic Director Vince Dooley) and President Adams (Georgia President Michael Adams), but I'm really working to please God. If I know all my

"If you know there's a Power that created you, that's much greater than you, that's never ending, you know you can tap into that resource that gives you peace and gives you hope instead of despair."

Richt's University of Georgia Football Program Mission Statement exemplifies this:

> To handle all responsibilities with excellence. To be dedicated to assisting our players to reach their full potential in the classroom, on the football field, and in society. Help them develop their body, mind, and spirit to the fullest. Be a great example of what we are trying to teach our players. Do not do anything that would destroy what we are trying to build. Honor God with all our actions.

CHAPTER THIRTEEN

TOM LEHMAN

Tom Lehman kept his perspective during a long journey from Minnesota and the mini-tours to the British Open and beyond. A late bloomer at each stage of his career—junior, amateur, and professional golf—Lehman was just learning to be a winner in one phase when it was time to move to the next. As a result, when he turned pro in 1982, he didn't have the confidence to make the normal progression that most tour stars do. It wasn't until 1992, after years of mini-tour play around the world, that he not only made it on the PGA Tour, but made it big.

In 1989, Lehman was practically broke. He had made no money to speak of as a golfer, pocketing just $80,000 over eight years in the late '80s and early '90s. He had decided to quit golf and get a job. Down to the last of their savings, Lehman and his wife, Melissa, decided to take one last chance, spending their final $300 on entering a tournament in South Africa. That last shot became a shot in the arm, as Lehman won $30,000, setting off a new sense of confidence and a complete turn-around of his game. Among the upper echelon of players throughout the 1990s, Lehman was named player of the year in 1996, when he won over $1.7 million. His career earnings now exceed $7 million.

It seems that $300 was a good investment.

"I wouldn't trade those years for anything," says Lehman. "I look back, and there's nothing but good memories. It was difficult. You really had to want to play golf and get good in order to go through it. You have got to do whatever it takes. So I look back at that and say, 'We did it.' Melissa and I together, we did whatever we had to do to get the job done. I just wanted to get as good as I could possibly get. I didn't care if I never got rich or famous. I wanted to play because I wanted to be good. And I always believed that I had the ability to be a really good player."

The lessons Lehman learned during the days he nearly quit have been put to good use after he established himself as a contender on the PGA Tour. "For a while, my entire life revolved around golf," Lehman says. "When I got my priorities straight, that changed."

"Maybe when you deal with failure for so long," Lehman says, "it tends to take a long time to overcome the idea you are a failure. The Hogan Tour [now Nike] was a huge step. Winning on the PGA Tour was another big step. Winning a major was the biggest step of all. So I see myself now as really being a champion. And yet, I know I am capable of being even better.

"A lot more people are going to go through the school of hard knocks than people who jump right in and are instant successes. Both ways are just fine. But I think more people can relate to going through some tough times before the good times. That is where you have to keep the balance in your life. You are a golfer, that's what you do. Obviously you want to be good, but there are things beyond golf that are far more important, and that is who you are on the inside."

And just who Lehman is on the inside has shown as he has dealt with the disappointment and pressure that comes with life on the Tour.

Four times in the '90s, Lehman played in the final group of the U.S. Open, attempting to win the coveted title. Four times, he watched someone else win. For Lehman, the Open is more like an open wound. During four consecutive summers—1995, 1996, 1997, and 1998—Lehman either held or shared the lead after three rounds. On each occasion, he ended up making a consolation speech to the media. Those experiences, combined with a similar heartbreaking loss at the Masters in 1994, left Lehman to deal with the disappointment of being one of the world's finest golfers who had never won a major tournament.

"That was always my greatest fear," Lehman said. "To die and have it written on my tombstone: *Here Lies Tom Lehman, He Couldn't Win The Big One.*"

All of which made the finish to the 1996 U.S. Open the backdrop for interesting drama. For the final round, Lehman was paired with his friend Steve Jones. They were deadlocked after 71 holes, two pals on a stroll that would reward only one. Jones shot 69 and looked to the heavens. Lehman shot 71 and looked to next year—again.

But it is what happened en route to the final score that typifies Lehman's outlook on his 0-for-Opens. It was Lehman who kept Jones—playing in his first major championship since the 1991 British Open—calm. He gave words of encouragement to Jones as they played together. He broke the ice as they walked down the first fairway.

"We walked off the first tee, and Tom said, 'Let's pray,'" says Jones. "So Tom prayed for both of us. And put his arm around me. And we prayed walking down the first hole. And he just basically said, 'You know, let's just glorify God today and give him this day.' And I said, 'Amen. Let's do it.'"

"I could tell he was a little bit nervous," says Lehman. "Something was really in my heart—you know, here we are, two believers in Jesus Christ—maybe this could be a real example today of what it means to be Christian athletes."

Twice during the round, as the pair talked between holes, Lehman encouraged Jones with a favorite Scripture.

"Tom and I were walking down the 16th fairway, and he shared with me Joshua 1:9, which was his verse for the year," says Jones.

> "Something was really in my heart . . . maybe this could be a real example today of what it means to be Christian athletes."

"I said, 'Jonesy, I want to share a verse with you,'" says Lehman. "And I shared with him, 'Be bold and strong. Banish fear and doubt, for the Lord your God is with you wherever you go.'"

"I needed that at that point," says Jones. "Because in the U.S. Open there's a lot of pressure. And anything can happen. He gave me the right focus. . .and it really relaxed me."

"If I saw Steve Jones just walking down the street at home, I would walk over, we'd talk, and I would say something nice to him," says Lehman. "If I could encourage him in some way, I probably would. So if we are playing the last round of the U.S. Open, it shouldn't be any different. It was just so he would know that no matter what happened throughout that entire day that God loved him, God was with him just like He is with everybody else."

"It was special to be with him that day," remembers Jones. "To be encouraging to me on the golf course when most guys would want to beat each other's brains out. You know, here we were, good friends out on the golf course, but yet being very competitive."

Lehman's words helped inspire Jones to his amazing win in what still remains the greatest day of his professional career.

"I was disappointed in myself, but I was extremely happy for Steve," Lehman says. "I really felt like the prayer that we prayed at the beginning—that we would honor God that day—that was answered."

Lehman's example of humility was startling to some, normal to Lehman. Yet, at the end of the day, he still had not won a major. He was beginning to wonder if his time would ever come. But golf's heartbreak kid was rewarded for his patience just one month after his loss to Jones at the 1996 U.S. Open.

Lehman won the 1996 British Open—the major he least expected to win—en route to being the Tour's leading money winner that year and being named Player of the Year.

Sometimes, even golf can be fair.

It was a highlight not only for Lehman, but also for the man he had encouraged just one month earlier.

"When he won at the British Open, it was as if I'd won it," remembers
Jones. "I was so happy for him, and I felt like I was a part of it. I'll never for-
get the joy I felt watching him win that tournament after going through what
I knew he felt at the U.S. Open and the Masters. It was just incredible."

"Steve, when I won the British Open, was one of the first people to call,"
recalls Lehman. "And he was so excited—and genuinely excited. You know,
there's sometimes when guys say, 'Hey, good job. I'm proud or happy for
you.' And that's like the right thing to say. . . . But you know, his excitement
was. . .straight from the heart. . .he knew how much it meant to me."

For Lehman, it was the realization of a dream and the release of worry
over the wording on his tombstone. Still, he has kept a clear perspective on
what winning a major means.

"I'm happy with what I've achieved," Lehman says. "But it's more
important for me to, to feel like I've been used. I think that's it. You know,
all my life to have been useful, to have meant something. You know, to have
affected other people's lives in a positive way. . .so that people, you know,
when I'm gone, will say, 'You know, I remember back when he did this. And
boy, it really changed my life.'" ■

CHAPTER FOURTEEN

LaDAINIAN TOMLINSON

There are a few elite athletes whose preeminence calls for them to be identified by their initials. In the National Football League, no such star shines brighter than the man known simply as LT.

LaDainian Tomlinson is the finest running back in pro football. He is a 5-foot-10, 220-pound ball of excitement who has the speed to run away from defenders and the power to run them over.

In football's new millennium, no player has been more productive or had greater value to his team than LT.

Over his first seven years in the league, Tomlinson's performance has ranked among the all-time great backs in the game. He recorded seven consecutive seasons of 1,200 or more yards rushing and pushed his career totals to 10,650 yards rushing and 115 touchdowns scored on the ground. Those career totals, through the 2007 season, already have him ranked 19th in rushing yards, 3rd in rushing touchdowns, and 7th in total touchdowns in league history. Entering the 2008 season, he was just two typical LT seasons away from a spot in the top five in rushing yards.

Incredibly versatile, LT has also caught 458 passes out of the backfield for an additional 3,375 yards and 14 touchdowns, making him one of the top receiving backs in NFL history. And he has completed 8 of 11 passes for 143 yards and 7 touchdowns. He is perhaps the player most feared by defenses around the league.

Tomlinson showed why that fear is real in 2006, when he was selected as the league's Most Valuable Player. That season, he ran for 1,815 yards and 28 touchdowns and broke the NFL's single-season scoring record with 31 total touchdowns scored. He racked up 2,323 total yards from scrimmage, the sixth-highest single-season total in league history, and set 13 new NFL records and 6 new team records. He obliterated the NFL's single-season scoring record of 186 points, which had stood in place since Paul Hornung established it way back in 1960.

In 2003, he not only rushed for over 1,600 yards but also caught 100 passes. He has totaled over 14,000 yards from scrimmage during his seven years, which places him on the verge of breaking into the top 10 in that category as well.

"The combination of his great athletic ability, his great strength, and his competitiveness allows him to play as big as he wants to."

His performance has almost single-handedly lifted the San Diego Chargers to among the league's elite teams and one of the most watched.

With so much achieved at this stage of his career, LT seems destined to go into the books as one of the all-time greats.

"I think when you mention him, you have to mention him with the great backs," said LT's fullback, Lorenzo Neal. "It's really a treat to play with him and to say I got to play with one of the great ones."

"You realize this is one of the greatest guys who has ever played, and using that term is a sum of all the things that he has accomplished," says Chargers' Head Coach Norv Turner. "But you see that every day with the plays he makes."

While Tomlinson's reputation is enormous, his stature is somewhat less than ideal for an NFL running back. Because of this, the power and authority with which he carries the ball can be surprising.

"The combination of his great athletic ability, his great strength, and his competitiveness allows him to play as big as he wants to," says Turner.

"It's pretty exciting because you never know what's going to happen," concurs Neal. "He puts on moves like I've never seen anyone else do…. He is Superman without a cape."

"A running back is unique because he has his own running style," says the ever-humble Tomlinson, deflecting personal praise.

It is that combination of humility and exceptional talent that has pushed Tomlinson to greatness. Never satisfied with his own performance, he consistently strives to reach a higher level. That work ethic made Tomlinson stand out in college. Considered by some to be too small to make a big impact, LT became the NCAA's leading rusher during both his junior and senior seasons at Texas Christian University. His performance garnered attention—he finished fourth in the Heisman Trophy voting as a senior and won the Doak Walker Award as the nation's top running back, despite his team's lack of visibility. He also caught the attention of NFL scouts, and the Chargers selected him with the fifth overall pick of the 2001 NFL draft.

But long before national acclaim and broken records, the life of this future superstar had the most humble of beginnings.

Miles from the spotlight of NFL fame, LaDainian was born in the tiny town of Rosebud, Texas. At six years old, he and his family moved to the central Texas city of Waco, where he eventually played high school football for the University High School Trojans.

The high school experience was practically

"Working with kids and working with the community has always been something that's dear to my heart."

divine for Tomlinson. On the football field, he rushed for over 2,500 yards and 39 touchdowns in his senior season in a performance that earned him all-state honors.

But his dream to play in the NFL began at a much younger age.

"The dream started when I was about five or six years old. I remember seeing the late, great Walter Payton playing," says Tomlinson. "He was definitely who I wanted to be like."

For LT, being like Payton meant more than making tacklers miss on the field. It also meant becoming personally involved in his community and using his platform to have an impact on others. Now, through his multiple outreaches to the San Diego community—much like his hero Payton—LT's commitment to helping others has become as much his trademark as his play on the field. It was only fitting that LaDainian received the Walter Payton NFL Man of the Year Award in 2006 for his example and commitment to others.

"Working with kids and working with the community has always been something that's dear to my heart," said Tomlinson. "So that's why I have football camps; my wife and I give out scholarships to kids going to college. We have a turkey drive. We have a toy drive at Christmas time. We bring groups to games, and we give them treats—they get hot dogs or sodas at the game, and we give school supplies. So we do little things like that to help kids."

The "little things" Tomlinson refers to are not quite so little. Through his Tomlinson Touching Lives Foundation, his impact has in fact been huge. The foundation, led by LT and his wife LaTorsha, hosts events throughout the year, including youth football camps in San Diego and Texas, a golf tournament, entrepreneurial training programs for students, a fishing trip for the homeless and at-risk teens in San Diego, a Thanksgiving program providing more than 1,000 San Diego families with complete holiday dinners, and a Christmas program in which they give away more than 1,500 holiday gifts to the patients at San Diego's Children's Hospital and Health Center. At each Chargers' home game, LT hosts The 21 Club, where he invites 21 kids from San Diego youth groups and nonprofit organizations to attend a game. After the game, LT invites the children down to the field where they get a one-on-one visit with him and a chance to pose for pictures. Each member of The 21 Club goes home with a goody bag filled with school supplies, books, and games.

The foundation also initiated the School Is Cool Scholarship Fund, which awards 30 annual scholarships to college-bound students based on academics, community involvement, and volunteerism. Of the 30 students selected by Tomlinson each year, 15 are selected from San Diego and 15 are chosen from LT's alma mater, University High in Waco.

Tomlinson takes the same approach to helping others as he does his success on the field; it seems it's not so much "What I have done,"but rather "What more can I do?"

"I always can do more; I always feel like I can do more," he says. "I feel like if I can touch someone at a critical time in their life, then I am doing something right."

And, it seems, LT is consistently doing the right thing. Whether in the community or on the field, it is clear to those around him that he is not thinking about himself. This attitude of sacrifice has elevated him to superstar status.

"When he goes out there, you know he's there for you and he's there to work; he's a team guy." says teammate Kassim Osgood. "And he's

always motivating people to work harder and to strive for success."

"It's not about him—it's about the team, and he shows up every day and follows the rules," says former Chargers' player and team chaplain, Miles McPherson. "He's not trying to break the ranks and get special treatment, and that sets the tone for everybody else on the team."

"It's about leading by example," says Chargers' Director of Public Relations. "He's always doing his best to be the best he can be, and with that example, he expects people around him to follow that and be the best they can be."

"I think I got my work ethic from my mama," Tomlinson states. "You know, I see her working two jobs, and I'll see her in the morning and I'll see her at night because throughout the day she was trying to make a living, putting food on the table. So I always felt like if my mom can work two jobs doing something she doesn't really like doing,

something that I like doing— playing football—why not work as hard as I possibly can in doing it and being the best I can possibly be."

For LT, being the best he can be starts with priorities, also instilled in him by his mother, Loreane.

"It's been faith, it's been his family, and then it's been football, and I would say in that order," says Johnston. "The confidence that he has, the way he leads by example, the course he follows, the dedication that he has to his family—they're all great examples of Christ."

"I think that's what carries him and his character—because of his belief and his faith in God," says Neal.

"I couldn't imagine if Christ was not in my life," Tomlinson says. "In fact, that's the number one thing my mother gave me, is leading me to Christ. . . . It's because of Christ I have direction. I know where I'm going, and I know how to get there.

"I absolutely know who I am playing for, because after the game when I take that knee in center field, and to thank God and everyone else like the opposite team, I know I am playing for Christ."

"LT will never be defined by the football player, but by the man that he is and the things that he stands for," Neal says. "To me he's a better man than a football player, and that's hard for people to imagine."

LaDainian's character and faith were severely put to the test early in 2007. Just five days after being named league MVP, Tomlinson and the Chargers were knocked out of the playoffs with a heartbreaking 24–21 defeat at the hands of the New England Patriots. It was the lowest point of his professional career.

But the sting of this loss would not compare to the devastating news LaDainian received just one month later. On February 23rd, LT's father, Oliver Tomlinson, and his older brother, Ronald McClain, were tragically killed in a single-car accident near Waco, Texas.

"It's easy to question, 'Why God, why did this happen?' but that's because of our own selfish reasons," said LaDainian. "We're looking at me instead of what's better for me and what God has in store for me. No matter what I'm going through, my faith in Christ gets me through — whatever situation may come up.

"Someone told me that we'll see our fathers again, and I know one thing he's going to ask me is, 'What did you do with my name?' One day I'm going to say, 'Pop, I did good by your name.'"

Millions of fans, admirers, teammates, and friends would undoubtedly, wholeheartedly agree. ▪

CHAPTER FIFTEEN

CURT SCHILLING

He is what is referred to in baseball as a "gamer."

He is baseball's consummate warrior—a pitcher who wants the ball in his hand for the big games, will play through pain, and demands excellence from himself. He is the type who will proverbially put the team on his back and carry them, who comes up with his biggest performances in the most important games.

He is also a bit of a maverick—outspoken to the point of admittedly being a lightning rod at times. He is not one to ever be concerned with being politically correct and is unafraid to speak his mind, and he is usually unconcerned about what the public will think of him when he does.

An imposing presence on the mound over his career, Curt Schilling is a workhorse in an era of pampered pitchers. Over his 20 years in the major leagues through the 2008 season, Schilling had thrown over 180 innings in each of the 11 seasons in which he was healthy and was a starting pitcher. He also averaged more than seven innings per start in every season he was in the starting rotation. And for much of that time, he was dominant.

Over his 3,200-plus innings in his career, Schilling averaged nearly a strikeout per inning, with 3,116 total, making him just the 13th pitcher to reach that standard. Among those 13, Schilling has the highest ratio of strikeouts to walks and is one of only four pitchers to have recorded his 3,000th strikeout before allowing 1,000 walks. He set a National League record for strikeouts by a right-handed pitcher with 319 in 1997. He has three 20-win seasons among his total of 216 career wins, a number that is somewhat misleading in that he

Schilling has been at his best in the postseason. In 12 different series—four division championship series, four league championship series, and four World Series—he has been nearly unbeatable. In 19 starts, he is 10–2 with a 2.23 ERA and 120 strikeouts in 133 innings.

In 2001, Schilling teamed with Randy Johnson to carry the Arizona Diamondbacks to the World Series championship. In a thrilling seven-game triumph over the New York Yankees, Schilling posted a microscopic ERA of 1.69 and shared Series MVP honors with Johnson.

Yet it was three years later that the legend of Curt Schilling was firmly etched into the baseball history books, with his performance for the Boston Red Sox in the 2004 World Series.

In one of the most vivid displays of courage in sports history, on October 19, 2004, Schilling persevered through an ankle injury to win Game Six of the 2004 ALCS against the New York Yankees in what is now known as the "Bloody Sock Game."

Schilling had torn a tendon in his right ankle two starts earlier. He attempted to pitch with the injury in Game One of the series. It didn't go well and was part of the reason the Red Sox found themselves down 3–0 to the Yankees.

No team had ever come back from a 3–0 deficit to win a championship series. But the Red Sox pulled out dramatic extra-inning victories in the fourth and fifth games to set up the dramatic Game Six.

Schilling's doctors suggested an experimental medical procedure in

Schilling campaigned for President George W. Bush in 2004, and for John McCain in 2008.

which the pitcher's tendon could be stitched to his skin—it was the only possibility of him pitching. The procedure had been tried before only on cadavers, and no one knew whether he would be able to put pressure on his ankle, let alone pitch.

When he strode to the mound in Yankee Stadium that night, he prayed. And then he just kept on throwing strikes. Blood oozed from the injury right from the beginning, and the national television audience continued to watch in amazement as close-ups showed both Schilling's bloodstained white sanitary sock and the grimace on his face as he pitched through the discomfort.

After seven incredible innings, and allowing only four hits, Schilling left the field with a bleeding suture and a 4–1 lead. The Red Sox held on to win and forced a Game Seven, in what would eventually be the greatest comeback in any postseason series in the history of baseball—all fueled by one of the game's most amazing individual performances.

After the game, Shilling told reporters, "I've got to say, I became a Christian seven years ago, and I never have been touched by God like I was tonight. I tried to go out and do it by myself in Game One, and you saw what happened. . . . Tonight was God's work tonight, no question. . . . God did something amazing. . . . I knew I wasn't going to be able to do this alone. And I prayed as hard as I could. I didn't pray to get a win or to make great pitches.

"I just prayed for the strength to go out there tonight and compete, and He gave me that.

"When I came out of the game after the seventh inning, I knew what I was going to say—win or lose," Schilling recalled. "Because I knew that I couldn't deny what I just experienced, which was the Lord saying, 'I am going to prove to you tonight, I am who I say I am.'"

When he was asked a follow-up question at the post-game press conference, Schilling responded again by sharing his amazement over what he had just been through. He told them, "I just wish everybody on this planet could experience the day I just experienced. Never use the words 'unbelievable' and 'Lord' in the same sentence. It's just the most amazing day of my life."

The response to his comments was mixed.

"When I made it known publicly that I was a believer—that I was a Christian—the media tends to go the other route," he said. "They tend to snicker and laugh about it, and it's unfortunate because I play something that's very significant to billions of people."

Still, many were touched by Schilling's genuineness. Most reporters who followed him at all already knew he was not one given to hyperbole, and they recognized his almost child-like acknowledgement of his faith.

"He said it differently," ESPN's Peter Gammons remembered. "Some guys don't mean to, but they make it sound as if God is cheering for them.

"I thought 'Schill' really defined what it is to be a Christian. You're not asking God to pick you over the other guy. You ask Him for the strength to go out and do whatever you can."

Schilling is emphatic that was the case. He said that when he went to the mound in Yankee Stadium for the bottom of the first inning for that game, with 50,000 Yankees fans booing him and his sutured ankle, he never felt calmer. And he knew why.

"It was such a peaceful feeling out there," Schilling said. "When you think about the environment, it sounds anything but peaceful. But I was relaxed. I was able to focus.

"I knew that the only other way you would understand what I went through is to be in my shoes. I had a change in my relationship with the

Lord in that 24-hour window that I can't talk about without getting emotional. What I went through mentally and where He got me—I never knew I could get there. I was the most relaxed person on the planet. I didn't know we were going to win, but I knew that how it went was how it was supposed to be played out, and I just wanted to be a part of it."

The win forced a Game Seven, making the Red Sox the first team in Major League Baseball history to come back from a three-games-to-none deficit. They went on to win Game Seven and the ALCS and to make their first World Series appearance since 1986.

A week later, Schilling took the hill to face the St. Louis Cardinals in Game Two of the World Series. Just minutes before the game, he still didn't know what he would be able to do, as the tendon had been re-stitched earlier that day.

Again he pitched well. Again there was blood oozing through his sock. Again the Red Sox won. They went on to sweep the Cardinals and with the World Series for the first time in 86 years.

After this one, Schilling told reporters, "If you haven't checked it out, read Philippians 4:13: 'I can do all things through Him who strengthens me' (NASB). I can't do anything these days without having that reverberate in my head."

Six more innings of scoreless ball with a tendon stitched to his skin, and Schilling became the nation's hero—not just Red Sox Nation, as the fan base is called, but an American hero for the fall of 2004.

"It's unbelievable," said Red Sox pitching coach Dave Wallace. "Look not only at the circumstances, but who he's doing it against. The Yankees and the Cardinals? Two of the best batting lineups in a long, long time. Amazing."

It was not the first time that Schilling's character was on display; just the first time the nation got to watch it play out.

Yet, a few years before his heroic World Series effort, Schilling showed what he was made of. It happened during his 2001 Series winning season in Arizona. What should have been one of the greatest years of his life became his most challenging. Early in the year, he learned his wife, Shonda, was battling a rare thyroid disease and a potentially deadly form of skin cancer.

In February of 2001, the normally energetic Shonda suddenly forgot how to get to common places like the grocery store and found herself dozing off in the middle of the day. She was diagnosed with an under-active thyroid that slowed her metabolism, and she was treated with medication. But while she was being observed, doctors discovered something else: a cancerous mole on her back.

She was diagnosed with malignant melanoma (skin cancer) and, in May of that year, underwent surgery to remove 25 potentially malignant moles. By June, she had endured four operations to diagnose more suspicious moles.

While Shonda endured her trial, Curt was determined he would not let his professional obligations get in the way of his responsibility to his family. So, every day during spring training that year, Schilling woke up at 4:00 a.m., kissed his wife and three young children goodbye, and made a two-hour commute from the family home in Phoenix to the Diamondbacks' training facility in Tucson.

Each afternoon, following practice or a game, he made the two-hour drive back. He was committed to be there for his wife.

"I felt I should be there during the hardest time," Schilling said. "There were all sorts of questions we had, and I wanted us to be together.... Sure, you get tired, but that's a small sacrifice to pay. When you get married, you take an oath: 'In sickness and in health.' It's a small price to pay."

Though he battled both physical and emotional exhaustion during the grueling seven-week period, Schilling kept his composure.

In 2008, Schilling underwent surgery for biceps tenodesis and to repair a torn rotator cuff and torn labrum.

"It's my job to take care of my family. What kind of message would I send to her (Shonda) or my children if I was an emotional wreck?"

Schilling recalled losing his father to a fatal aortic aneurysm 13 years earlier—just months before Curt made his Major League debut. He was determined to do as much as possible within his control to not lose his wife or create uncertainty in the family.

Following the events of 2001, additional masses were discovered in Shonda's breast and groin areas, but they have not been cancerous. Since then, she has been under regular monitoring—but for now, she has beaten cancer.

The experience ingrained in Schilling the realization that every day is a gift in which he must make the most of his time with his wife. His sacrifice was simply a natural response.

"She's my best friend. She's always been there for me to lean on, and I wanted to be there for her."

Schilling's perspective has radically changed from his early days in the big leagues. He was a 21-year-old with an attitude, a red-and-blue-streaked mohawk, an earring, a flashy Corvette, and a reputation as an off-the-mound crazy man. Then Orioles' manager Frank Robinson had an early influence, as did Roger Clemens. However, the event that Schilling says truly turned him around occurred one day in 1997 while he was in the midst of a successful season with the Philadelphia Phillies.

"I was driving home from the ballpark and thinking about how tired I was of waking up every morning with no real aim in my life," Shilling said. "We had our first kid, and I also wanted a foundation for my family. . . . While I was driving, I said the Lord's Prayer. I waiting for thunder and lightning, and that never came, but my outlook on the world changed."

For Schilling, the change—while gradual—has been profound. It has molded him into the man he is today, epitomized by the spirit he showed in the Bloody Sock games and in caring for his ailing wife.

"I realize the lessons in everything, even losing, and can take away something about better preparation or the need for humility," he said. "It becomes a lot easier to live with yourself. The losses are no less painful, but I know now the difference between failure and non-success.

"You work as hard as you can with what God gives you. You fail only if you quit."

CHAPTER SIXTEEN

TIM HOWARD

Tim Howard made an improbable jump to major league sports.

He went straight from high school in his hometown of North Brunswick, New Jersey, directly to Major League Soccer where he was allocated to the New Jersey MetroStars. He quickly became the best keeper in the MLS for two seasons and made nine appearances for the U.S. National Team, where he was groomed as the goalkeeper of the future.

Then on July 14, 2003, Howard signed a four-year contract with Manchester United, becoming the first American to play in goal for what has been called the world's most important sports franchise.

Catapulted from the relative obscurity of a New Jersey team to world football's most visible stage, Howard found himself playing against the greatest players in the world in front of the world's most demanding fans.

"It's a difficult task," Howard said. "You have to stay focused, and I think the ability to focus sets a good goalkeeper apart. You know you have these guys to your back—you have 20,000 right behind you—they're going to help you stop the shot, so you go out and you be confident."

In his first season with United, Howard registered 16 clean sheets en route to being named the Premier League's best keeper by the Professional Footballer's Association. He had a perfect record in 10 of his first 15 appearances during his first United season.

In 2004, Howard became the first American to win an FA Cup medal and was voted Goalkeeper of the Year by the other Premier League players. While he did not stay with United beyond 2006, moving to another Premier League team, Howard became a celebrity in Europe.

In Howard's prior life on the other side of the Atlantic, he was rarely recognized. Occasionally, a "soccer mom" with a couple of kids would notice him as a professional player. In his new life, the American-born and bred goalie couldn't walk down the street without people nudging each other, whispering, and asking for autographs.

Howard's success in such a high pressure situation became even more impressive when it became known that he suffers from a misunderstood and often misdiagnosed neurological disorder.

Howard was born with a condition called Tourette's syndrome (TS), a neurological disorder characterized by rapid tics and vocalizations. He was first diagnosed with TS when he was 11 years old. Instead of it interfering with his playing sports, sports actually helped him control his symptoms.

"When I was 10 years old, I had some interesting things going on with me physically—tics if you will," said Howard. "My family didn't know what it was, but they knew their son had something different about him.

"I don't speak about Tourette's syndrome as a negative thing because I can't. My life has been so blessed because of TS. I have been able to reach out to children who have it—hundreds of kids. I've been able to share my story with them and give them some inspiration and hope.

"The Lord in turn has given me a platform in soccer—Manchester United, the New York MetroStars, the U.S. National Team, the list goes on and on—and these are big names that draw attention, and I'm able to speak out and say, 'This isn't a bad thing.'"

Not only did Howard persevere through Tourette's as a child, he also grew up in a home without a father.

"I came from a family of separated parents..... Things were tough," said Howard. "Money was tight, my parents worked. My mom worked two jobs to make ends meet. She was an awesome inspiration to me at a really young age. You know, she never really complained. She had a lot to complain about, but she never really complained. She put her nose to the grind(stone) and got it done. I never went to school without shoes; I never went to bed hungry. I certainly could have, but she was a trooper."

If Howard's rise seems like a fairy tale, then his life could be scripted as a classic success story.

His road to the top wasn't typical, which goes along with his character. Howard is an atypical young man, especially for an athlete of his caliber. He exemplifies humility in a time when ego usually takes precedence. He's driven and focused, yet humble and kind.

"I like to think of myself as humble," Howard said. "I think that as human beings we all have an ego inside of us. To go from where I was, which was good, and being elevated to Manchester United, it was just so far gone that I couldn't comprehend something like that. That had to be bigger than me."

To avoid being caught up in the trappings of fame and fortune, Howard has chosen to place his focus on his family and his faith. His passion is to excel at the sport he loves. Still, his undying devotion is not to a game, but rather to the One who gave him the ability to play the game.

"To me it's important to keep my priorities straight as a football player and that's to keep God first," Howard said. "And playing in front of 70,000 people, but also as a child of God and knowing Jesus is everything for me."

CHAPTER SEVENTEEN

TONY DUNGY

The road to the Super Bowl is paved with broken dreams, where champions are determined by their character and ability to overcome adversity.

In both 2003 and 2004, the Indianapolis Colts believed Super Bowl glory was theirs to be had. Each season they had won 12 regular season games and the AFC South division championship en route to the playoffs.

Yet, each time, their Super Bowl dreams were derailed by their conference nemesis, the New England Patriots.

Football experts began to suggest that the Colts were a great team that simply did not have what it took to become a champion. They questioned the heart of quarterback Peyton Manning and the tenacity of coach Tony Dungy.

But in the 2006 season, Dungy and his Colts proved the skeptics wrong. Powered by an explosive offense and a rebuilt defense, the Colts won the world championship with a Super Bowl XLI victory over the Chicago Bears 29–17.

With the victory, Dungy became the first ever African-American coach to win a Super Bowl.

Tony Dungy knows success. During his tenure in Indianapolis, Dungy has been one of the most successful coaches in the NFL. Through 2007, he had become the only coach in Colts' history to post six consecutive seasons with 10 or more wins and a playoff appearance. Entering the 2008 season, Dungy had taken nine straight teams to the playoffs, tying Tom Landry's streak (1975–83) for the most consecutive playoff appearances by a head coach since the

1970 NFL Merger. Along with Dungy, only five other coaches in history have won 100 or more regular-season games in their first 10 years as a head coach.

But winning is only part of Tony Dungy's legacy. He is known by those who have played for him, coached with him, and competed against him as one of the classiest men in all of sport.

In Indianapolis, his players love the atmosphere he has created.

"It's fun to come to work each day when you have great guys to work with," said tight end Dallas Clark.

"A lot of guys say he's a player's coach because he's played the game and understands the rest of the guys' needs."

"It's finding what will work," said Takik Glenn, who played offensive tackle for the Colts from 1997–2006. "It's not a negative atmosphere. Coaches are more encouraging than degrading, and that's abnormal in a football atmosphere."

That philosophy has been Dungy's since he arrived. And while different from the approach of many coaches, it has obviously been successful.

"We had a blueprint," says Dungy. "I knew what the final product looked like and never deviated from that. I just had to stay patient as we built it."

"When he first got here, all he talked about was expectations," said Glenn. "He talked about how we do things and buying into the system."

"Tony's philosophy from when he came in was to get players here to win, we need to learn how to win. We need to learn how to play big games, and this will grow," said center Jeff Saturday. "I think he's done a great job of just showing if you play the position you're supposed to play, you play the fundamentals and the techniques you're supposed to do, it doesn't matter who you are or where you're from, any guy can fit into our system and make it work."

"It's just a matter of getting the right players, the right style of guys, teaching them, and having them feel comfortable that they know their assignments and know what to do," says Dungy, ever deflective of the praise. "We didn't get the results that we wanted right away, but no one was ready to be benched and everybody felt that it was a matter of time."

"He's a great leader; he explains everything to the guys," said linebacker David Thornton, who played for Dungy from 2002–2005. "He has such a thorough way that makes it easier to understand and for guys to respond and (say) 'I'm willing to work for him.'"

"He talks when he needs to talk, and when he talks, you listen," added Clark. "That's what I respect about him, and you respect that about your coach and you know he knows what he's talking about and he's a smart man."

"A lot of guys say he's a player's coach because he's played the game and understands the rest of the guys' needs," Thornton agreed. "But at the same time, his demeanor and the way he approaches guys' game—I think everyone responds really well and guys respect him. They respect him for the type of man he really is."

Dungy built this team by bringing in players and coaches who are men of character. Following an unconventional approach, he has passed over some more physically gifted prospects in the draft. Instead, he has chosen playmakers; players who may not have had the external tangibles that many scouts wanted but came up big in big games for major universities. More than that, Dungy has

> "I try to make it a positive environment where guys can learn and guys can grow,"

looked for young men of good character. He understood that if he could get the kinds of people who would grasp his philosophy, he could build a championship team.

He also knew that he could have an influence on his players that transcended the game.

"He's a great person and a great coach," said former defensive tackle Josh Williams, who played for Dungy from 2000–2005. "Family comes first, and he models that. He takes his kids to school before he comes to work. Just things like that. Everyone respects him and plays for him in a different way. He's like a father."

Dungy's approach has worked, because his players have seen his consistency each day. Whether after a win or a loss, in adversity, during poor practices, or after a contract extension, his character never changes.

"Every day he shows up, and he's the same Tony Dungy," said Saturday. "He's not gonna get

mad, he's not gonna scream at guys, he's not gonna yell."

"He's always the same, no matter what happens, and it kind of attaches to you," added Williams. "Guys grab a hold of that, and I think it rubs off on guys—it's rubbed off on me."

"I try to make it a positive environment where guys can learn and guys can grow," says Dungy.

"When you buy into the philosophy that. . .we have to encourage one another and believe in one another, and if we do that, we can be successful," states Glenn.

Dungy's approach has carried over into games, in even the most stressful of situations. His players have noticed how he has handled the pressure.

"If you see your coach not really getting rattled, not really responding to adversity in the wrong way—always keeping a positive attitude, always stressing about keeping a positive attitude—it definitely plays a factor in the way the players respond," said Thornton.

"I'm not going to belittle people, I'm not going to skirt the rules, I'm not going to use profanity," Dungy said. "Those are just the things that I was raised (in), and that's not going to change whether I'm a football coach or in another profession."

His relational approach has engendered loyalty from his players, who feel they have the best environment in the NFL.

"You obviously want to win for the team, but it's easier to do that when you have a coach like Coach Dungy leading the team—I mean, you want to win for him," says Clark.

"We hear all the time people who are disheartened with their current situation and they'll be like, 'Man you guys have got it great.' And they don't even play—they've just heard," says punter Hunter Smith.

In the eyes of his players, Tony Dungy is set apart by his faith—a faith that speaks louder in action than in words to those who watch him on a daily basis.

"At the end of the day, Coach Dungy's a man of God," said Smith. "He is a Christ-like man, and he coaches a team as Christ would coach a team. It's seldom been done and, in my opinion, never been done with the effectiveness and the commitment he does."

"Anyone can say things, but are you living it, are you bearing fruit? Is your life an example? Are you following Christ as He walked?" added Williams. "I really believe that's how he lives, and it shows."

"He sets a tone," says assistant coach Jim Caldwell. "I think you'll find that every one of us has become a better father being around him."

"You do try to model for them what you believe—and I don't get on my soapbox very often and talk about Christianity in the locker room," said Dungy. "I'll tell some stories from the Bible if I want to make a point about something to the team about something that happened that week.

"I don't tell them how to live or what to do, but I try to be myself and show Christ, and I think that's important. I think my job as a coach is more than just instructing guys on how to block or how to tackle."

"If you read about Jesus—so many of His lessons, so many of His character traits, just so much of who He was—you see that in Coach Dungy and how he coaches his team," said Smith.

Dungy's journey to a spot among the NFL coaching elite has been one of patience and perseverance. A record-setting quarterback at the University of Minnesota in the 1970s, he was considered too small to play that position in the NFL. Undrafted, Dungy signed as a free agent with the Pittsburgh Steelers in 1977 and made the team as a backup safety.

In his rookie year, when injuries struck the Steelers' first two quarterbacks, Dungy moved over to the other side of the ball for part of a game and became the only player in modern NFL history to both throw a touchdown pass and intercept a pass in the same game.

As a nickel-back, he played a key role on the Steelers' team that won Super Bowl XIII.

He began his coaching career in 1980, working his way from the college ranks to the NFL, becoming one of the game's best defensive coordinators. He was mentioned for numerous head coaching jobs over the years, but didn't get his chance until 1996

With the Super Bowl XLI victory over the Chicago Bears 29–17, Dungy became the first ever African-American coach to win a Super Bowl.

when the Tampa Bay Buccaneers hired him. While the wait was difficult, Dungy does not regret the process.

"God's timing is so different from ours," Dungy relates. "I'm
happy to have waited 15 years to become a head coach. When you
achieve something after some near misses, after some disappoint-
ments, it makes it much sweeter than if it comes right away—there's
no doubt about it."

In Tampa, Dungy turned one of the NFL's worst franchises into a
consistent winner—a standard he has upheld in Indianapolis. At the
heart of his drive to excellence is his commitment to win—and win
the right way—while having a positive impact on the community.

"I told Jim Irsay. . .'Hey, I want to come, and we want to win a
Super Bowl for you and the City of Indianapolis, but if that's all we
do, if we just win, it'll be very, very shallow,'" Dungy recalls.

"I want to come, and I want to win, and I want to show people
that we can win, and I want to win with all the right type of guys.
And I want every mom and every dad in the state of Indiana, if their
son looks up to one of our guys, we're happy about it, we don't
care who they pick out of our team—all of our guys are outstanding
guys—and we're going to win the right way with high quality guys.
And I think that's what it's all about in coaching.

"Sure, we're judged by winning and you have to, and that's why
you're hired, but it's more than that. And to be effective, you want to
mold a team that the whole state can be proud of."

For Dungy, such desire is a natural outgrowth of his faith in God.
His faith is not a "good luck charm" or a crutch. It is a daily recog-
nition of his need for God and the realization of what is truly most
important in life.

"Playing football is great, and winning the Super Bowl is great, but it's not the most important thing in the world," he says. "Christ has shown me that athletics is a tool.

"There's a verse in the Bible that I really like—Matthew 16:26. It says, 'What will it profit a man if he gains the whole world and forfeits his soul?' I've seen that happen so many times in my football career. I've played with guys who are in the Football Hall of Fame. I've played with some of the greatest players ever to play. And you would think that if everyone had everything—money, the notoriety, the lifestyle, all the fun that you can have—but it doesn't last (if) that's all there is. It can be just as fleeting as you'd never believe. But the guys that I played with and experienced that true Christian bonding with? Those guys had that happiness no matter what the score, no matter the injuries—nothing could take that joy away."

That perspective is ultimately what connects Dungy and many of his players to the outside world. His faith was perhaps never quite so real to observers as when the world watched him go through his own personal agony.

On December 22, 2005, Dungy and his wife Lauren lived a parent's worst nightmare when they learned their eldest son, 18-year-old James, had been found dead in his suburban Tampa, Florida, apartment. His death was eventually ruled a suicide.

Because of his faith, Dungy has been able to endure the seemingly unbearable pain. It is said that great coaches have the ability to view the game differently. It is also said that men of great character have an ability to view the challenges of life with a different perspective. Dungy has done just that.

In the immediate aftermath of James' death, Dungy displayed dignity and grace. He was determined not to wallow in the pain, but to embrace the situation and see what lessons came from it—for him and for others.

"The day it happened," Dungy's younger son Eric recalls, "he was sad, but he wasn't a wreck or anything. He just kept his faith in God."

"The only word I can think of to describe it is 'extraordinary,'" Colts' General Manager Bill Polian told the media in the weeks following James' death.

Dungy believed that God placed him in the unenviable position of experiencing the situation for a higher purpose. He determined that through their pain, his family could be an example for others.

Many times in the past, Dungy had reached out to players and coaches who had experienced difficulties. Now, his very words were being tested on himself. He remained steadfast.

"The Lord has a plan," Dungy said. "We always think everything is going to be perfect for us, and it may not be that way, but it's still His plan. A lot of tremendous things are going to happen—it just may not be the way you see them.

"You may not win the Super Bowl. Your kids may not go on to be doctors and lawyers, and everything may not go perfectly. That doesn't mean it was a bad plan or the wrong thing. It's just like a football season. Everything's not going to go perfect. You're going to have some losses that you're going to have to bounce back from and some things that are a little unforeseen that you're going to have to deal with. It's how you work your way through things."

Dungy saw this firsthand as he communicated with fathers and mothers, brothers, sisters, and grandparents through letters, email, and phone calls since the tragedy. Each has a story to tell of what they are going through; each hoping the coach will have some words of wisdom to share.

"That's the encouraging thing, that I can say to people now that you'll make it," Dungy says.

Unwavering in his trust, Tony Dungy has displayed remarkable peace in the most difficult of personal circumstances. He remains unshaken.

"I don't know that we will ever really have any answers," he says of the "why" question he has asked regarding James. "We've heard from a lot of people, who have been in the same situation, and you never really know for sure. And so we've just tried to look forward and move forward and not really look back too much and search for answers.

"You think about, 'Could I have done something different? What if, what if, what if?' You look behind you, but there's nothing really you can change.

"I've said all along that God is in control," Tony Dungy says. "I have to believe that He's in control here, too."

What Dungy won't change is the quality time he commits to his family, refusing to let football get in the way. He takes his children to school in the morning and leaves the office early whenever he can. No sleeping in the film room for him. He continues to put his family first.

And so, he presses on with a commitment to turn pain into purpose and an ongoing passion for bettering each life he comes in contact with.

"I know in my heart that James' death has benefited many people, and that helps me feel better," he says.

"Because of Christ's love, I have peace in the midst of something very painful. I know how powerful His spirit is and I know that He can change people." ■

CHAPTER EIGHTEEN

JOHN SMOLTZ

The 1996 Cy Young Award winner, and the winningest post-season pitcher in baseball history, Atlanta Braves right-hander John Smoltz has been recognized as one of baseball's finest pitchers. . .when he has stayed healthy.

Arm problems have plagued Smoltz throughout his career, nearly bringing it to a premature end on more than one occasion. After blowing out his elbow for the third time, Smoltz underwent reconstructive surgery, known in baseball circles as "Tommy John" surgery, in March 2000. His future was uncertain.

After sitting out 14 months, Smoltz returned to the Braves' rotation in 2001. But his elbow could not handle the strain, and after just 25 innings, he was once again shut down for the season.

Smoltz had just 25 innings and as many trips to the disabled list as victories (two) to show for those two seasons. His career was at a crossroads. Braves brass felt that when Smoltz came back at the end of the 2001 season, the best chance of maximizing his health would be to put him in the bullpen and make him the team's closer. Smoltz agreed it would be the best way to work him back into his former role. So over the final two months of the 2001 season, Smoltz relieved Braves management by becoming a dominant closer, saving 10 of 11 games in which he pitched. The future suddenly held promise.

With his contract up in the off-season, Smoltz fielded offers from a number of teams promising to return him to the starting rotation. The Braves wanted him to stay in Atlanta, but now as the permanent closer.

But along with the closing—rather than starting—position, Atlanta offered him less money than the other teams.

In the end, Smoltz chose to stay home, embrace the role change, and make less money. It was a refreshing display of humility, loyalty, and priority from a bona fide star.

"It was the most complicated and hardest decision I've ever had to make," Smoltz says. "I talked with a lot of friends. I consulted my family. I prayed about it. All of the answers that I got led toward staying here.

"Sure, there was more money and there were more situations that on the outside, the world looks at like, 'You fool!' But I've never chased the money, and I've never been a person that would make my decisions solely on the world's view or the easy way out."

Ultimately, Smoltz's decision came down to what was best for the others in his life and what would bring ultimate fulfillment.

"It was a tough decision. Family had a lot to do with it, as well as all the community work, charity work. I'm involved in a Christian school, and that was a big part of it. I think people think that the (money) number is the only issue that matters and that could get you happiness, and it doesn't work that way. I was flattered and enjoyed the opportunity of seeking somebody else if it didn't work out here, but I'm glad it did."

The starter turned closer was dominant in his first full season in that role in 2002, setting a National League record by converting 55 saves, just two shy of the Major League mark. He again made the All-Star team and was a runner-up for the Cy Young Award. In 80 innings, he allowed only 59 hits and posted 85 strikeouts. He finished the season with a 3–2 record and a 3.25 ERA. Over the final two-thirds of the season, as he settled into his role, he was nearly unhittable.

At age thirty-four, a star was reborn, as was a career.

Smoltz enjoyed a long reign as the National League's most effective closer through 2004, when he was returned to the starting rotation. Another arm injury sidelined him in 2008, but it was not before he became the only pitcher to record 200 wins and 300 saves in a career. And even after his longtime pitching buddies Greg Maddux and Tom Glavine left to play elsewhere, Smoltz remained a Brave and has never looked back.

"I'm happy." says Smoltz. "I've always wanted to end my career in (the) Atlanta Braves. And I have that opportunity, and my family's happy, and I hope the Braves are happy."

In this case, "happy" would be an understatement. ■

CHAPTER NINETEEN

MICHAEL REDD

In August of 2005, Milwaukee Bucks All-Star guard Michael Redd signed a six-year, $91 million dollar deal to stay with the Bucks. Many considered it odd that Redd, one of the most prolific scorers in the game, decided to stay in Milwaukee and play for a team that had not been competitive. Yet for Redd, it was about more than just money or greener pastures.

For Redd, staying in Milwaukee meant continuing to invest himself in the community and to stay relatively close to his parents, who live in Ohio. It also meant he felt he had not yet arrived as a player and needed to continue to work on improving.

Taken with the 43rd pick in the 2000 draft, Redd is an oddity—a second-round pick who has become a star. A dynamic scorer, he has steadily grown into one of the NBA's top shooters, finishing each of his first seven seasons by raising his scoring average each year until 2007–08, when he averaged 22.7 points per game. His career-high average was 26.7 points in 2006–07, and he turned in a career- and franchise-high 57-point game in 2006.

Redd was an All-Star in 2004 and set a league record with eight 3-pointers in one game in 2006. Not bad for a player who once caused many scouts to question his outside shooting ability.

"I wasn't a shooter in college," said Redd. "The M.O. on me was that 'he's a slasher, a guy that likes to get to the rim.' But when you get to the NBA, it's a little bit more challenging to get to the rim. So what I had to do was work on my jump shot. . . . In order for me to play I had to learn how to shoot the basketball.

"I think I just worked at it, continually worked at it. Just worked at it, and worked at it, and worked at it until my arm almost fell off. I was determined to be a good 3-point shooter in the NBA.

"And that's the one thing I try to pride myself in, is having a great work ethic, staying an extra hour at the gym when practice is over, staying an extra half hour of shooting and working on my game."

The work paid off as Redd is now one of the most feared offensive players in the NBA. His shooting ability also was the main reason he was a member of the 2008 U.S. Olympic team that won gold at the Beijing Olympic games.

Still, Redd has made it clear that his career is about more than accolades and accomplishments.

"Basketball, it's not who I am," says Redd. "After everything is said and done, after I retire, I want people to say that he loved God more than anything else—(more) than he was an All-Star or he won championships, Michael Redd really loved God and really represented Christ. So you know basketball is what I love to do, but it's not everything to me. I value my faith and I value my family more than basketball."

Nowhere is that philosophy more evident than in Redd's hometown of Columbus, Ohio. It is here that Redd took a large portion of that contract extension money and built a church for his father.

"I try to carry myself in a Christ-like manner, always trying to stay representative of Him."

Redd is the son of a preacher. His father, James, taught him both a passion for basketball and an abiding faith. The father taught the son how to play and how to pray.

So, Michael gave back. He bought a prime piece of real estate on the east side of Columbus just a few months before his father's fiftieth birthday. A few months later, The Philadelphia Deliverance Church of Christ became a reality. It is a pristine house of worship, with stained glass windows, a soaring steeple, and a spacious auditorium that seats 500. It is also a symbol of thanks—a gift from a grateful son to his father. It is also the fulfillment of a childhood promise Redd made.

"Well, my dad's my role model and my hero," said Redd. "To see what he's gone through to be a full-time dad, to be a full-time pastor, and to be a full-time husband—those are the things I value and look to as a role model.

"My dad has taught me everything I know as far as life and basketball. We still talk. . . all the time and have a wonderful relationship.

"I really respect my father as a pastor, because being a pastor is not an easy thing to do. To see him do that for so many years, as well as work for his family, as well as being a good father and a good husband. . . . Hopefully I can be a good father like him one day."

It's clear he is on his way to that goal. Redd is an uncommon athlete—a humble man, whose life and career truly reflect his priorities.

"I try to carry myself in a Christ-like manner, always trying to stay representative of Him," Redd says. "And you know, I think in doing that, you automatically become a good role model to people.

"A lot of kids are influenced and impacted by our game and they tend to sway to what they see. So if you're having a good representation of yourself, they'll swing towards the good rather than the bad." ■

CHAPTER TWENTY

RON HUNTER

Did you hear the one about the college basketball coach who went barefoot during a game? He bared his SOUL.

OK, so while the pun may be weak, the coach's move was anything but.

Ron Hunter, the head basketball coach for Indiana University-Purdue University Indianapolis, went barefoot during a game on January 25, 2008 to raise awareness for needy children in Africa.

The move inspired donations of 110,000 pairs of shoes, which, along with a $20,000 gift, were donated to the Charlotte, North Carolina non-profit organization, Samaritan's Feet. In the summer of 2008, the shoes were then given to children in need around the world.

When Hunter first came up with the idea, his goal was to collect 40,000 pairs of shoes in honor of the 40th anniversary of the death of Dr. Martin Luther King, Jr. So, he coached the entire game against Oakland University without shoes. Some fans in attendance also went barefoot.

Hunter was moved by the outpouring of support, saying, "When we started this, I thought 40,000 was going to be tough. When they told me before the game we already had 100,000, honestly, I almost broke down in tears."

The coach appeared on several television and radio shows to pitch his idea and encourage others to join him. Soon the likes of Converse, Wal-Mart, Nine West, and the Department of Homeland Security all jumped in. The actions resulted in more than 100,000 children around the world receiving what may have been their first pair of shoes, all because one man had an idea and decided to act on it.

"There are hundreds of millions of children who don't have shoes," Coach Hunter said of the effort. "They suffer from diseases, infection, and many other ailments because they don't have shoes to wear. Needless to say, they can't play sports without shoes.

"We have been given an incredible opportunity and platform as coaches to use our status as role models for others and help children in need."

The coach, who almost never sits when coaching, said his feet were definitely sore after the game, but that only served to inspire him further.

"My feet hurt so bad," he said after the game. "But imagine a child or a human going their whole lives without shoes." ■

CHAPTER TWENTY-ONE

JOE GIBBS

It is rare to find a sports franchise that focuses on anything other than winning. But at Joe Gibbs Racing(JGR), while there is an absolute commitment to becoming a champion, winning is not the sole purpose of the franchise.

That fact is apparent when one first walks through the front door of JGR's facilities in Huntersville, North Carolina. The following mission statement is posted on the main wall of the entryway in large letters to make it stand out:

Our goal is to field for our sponsors and fans competitive race cars on a consistent basis with the goal of winning races and championships. Our expectation is that we will be able to see in our growth and success, things that would never have been accomplished except by the direct intervention of God.

Joe Gibbs Racing has a clearly defined purpose in which growth and excellence are the desired goals. God is at the center of their mission statement because Gibbs believes that is priority one.

In determining to build a team that way, Gibbs has mirrored the strategy upon which he built a championship NFL team, the Washington Redskins. As in football, Gibbs has built a champion on the track.

When the Gibbs Racing team captured the 2000 Winston Cup season championship, the media began immediately to ask Gibbs and his team what it felt like to be champions and whether or not they could repeat it in 2001.

"It's one thing to win one," Gibbs said of his championship season. "The hardest struggle in pro sports is to stay there. There are two things that kill great teams. One is adversity. There are a lot of people. . .they can deal with winning, but when you hit them with real hard things, they fall apart. The second thing is success. Most people can't deal with success."

Gibbs is at peace with his own personal struggle with the "S-word," in that he has gained perspective on what success truly entails.

He says, "Really, I think the only way we can have peace is to know that God loves me, He knows what's in my life, He's sealed me, I belong to Him, and in the end everything's going to work out the best for me.

"The great thing
about being a
Christian and
knowing God is in
charge is (that) I
think, 'I was going
through all that
for a purpose.'"

"The great thing about being a Christian and knowing God is in charge is (that) I think, 'I was going through all that for a purpose,'" says Gibbs. "Adversity normally can make you even better and propel you for years in the future. No matter what the problems are, He's bigger than any of them, and He'll kind of guide you through."

With a winning attitude for Gibbs Racing also came an attitude adjustment for Gibbs. He recognized he had, to a great extent, abandoned his role as father during his years coaching the Washington Redskins. So, he knew he had to change the way he went about his daily routine. Owning a stock car team provided for that change.

"My role is different," says Gibbs. "In football, I was a coach. I hands-on made things happen, called the plays, designed the plays. Over here, that's not my job. I couldn't do that if I wanted to. My role has changed. Now, by being an owner in auto racing, my job is to get the sponsors, pay the bills — which is a big deal — and to pick the people. I enjoy the change, really."

Although Gibbs remains as competitive as he ever was, he now enjoys other things besides victories. His children and grand-children are near the top of his list.

"It gives you a little bit different perspective," says Gibbs. "I think when you're young.... you're—and I certainly was—caught up in being successful, financially and vocationally. Then, a little bit later on, what kicks in is that you realize that isn't the only thing I need to be successful in to be successful in life."

Gibbs admits he overlooked those areas when he coached in the NFL. He doesn't like to look at photos of his sons, J.D. and Coy, when they were younger because it reminds him that he missed much of their childhood. It was not uncommon for Gibbs to become so engrossed in his work preparing for Sunday's opponent that he slept at the Redskins' offices and went days without seeing his family.

Now, he sets aside quality time for each of his sons and their chil-dren and looks for ways to involve family members in the business.

When he first made the jump from football to auto racing, he was determined to find a way for his sons to work with him in the venture. Gibbs remembered the toll his NFL coaching career took on the two, and he vowed his job would not come between them again. Now, both sons are involved day-to-day in the Gibbs Racing empire.

J.D. splits time between the front office and the track. He serves as president of Joe Gibbs Racing, overseeing much of the day-to-day operation of the team. He also drives for his dad in the NASCAR Craftsman Truck Series. Coy Gibbs also drives for his dad in the NASCAR Craftsman Truck Series. He had previously served in a variety of capacities for the Gibbs team.

"I think a dream for any par-ent would be that you could work with your kids," says Joe Gibbs. "Certainly this has been a

real thrill because of having J.D.
working here in the race shop with
me and Coy up the street. We all
see each other every day. We live
within 10 minutes of each other."

"This is the first business that
we've ever really run," says J.D.
"I came straight out of school
when we started this up, so we
didn't know really how to run it
any other way. So we just kind of
did what felt right, and it turned
out to be a pretty neat situation. Obviously, I am part of the
Gibbs family; that does help out
some. It helped especially getting a job here. But as far as the
overall team aspect, we've grown
so fast—from 15 members when
we first began to now over 100
employees. It's grown fast, but as
long as we keep the family concept, it makes it a lot easier."

"Getting to enjoy something—
when you think about it, how hard
is that?" asks Joe rhetorically.
"Something that everybody in the
family would enjoy—working
on racing and then to build a

business and a race team—it's very unusual. We're probably one of the luckiest families in the world to get an opportunity to do this.

"It's a little like going back to high school football again. You go on Friday nights and Saturday nights to watch J.D. and Coy race. You get caught up in it, and it's the same feeling, you know. You want them to do well. It breaks your heart when they don't."

"I couldn't think of driving for anyone else or working for anyone else besides him," says J.D. "It's great to have the father-son relationship away from business, but adding work to it brings kind of a new dimension to it. And who knows, years down the road, if things are still working out, I think it could be a great situation if I could keep driving for him."

Gibbs remains true to his strategy and principles of leadership. At Joe Gibbs Racing, it's not about Joe Gibbs, but rather it's about the team. Gibbs is clearly focused on people.

As the man in charge at Joe Gibbs Racing, Joe understands the weight of his role. "There's a big responsibility when you've got 60 families that have come to work for you," says Gibbs. "I want their job to be the best—our benefits and all the things we offer, our bonus programs, the work environment, the things we offer for the entire family.

"We try and have a lot of things where we involve the wives," says Gibbs. "We have a once-a-month get-together, where the wives try and come together and get an opportunity to do things together. And then we have different kinds of seminars, Bible studies, what have you, that the entire family can be a part of."

For it to be a team that everyone feels a part of, the Gibbs Racing Team has to walk the talk. And in a highly competitive atmosphere, they have done just that. In NASCAR many teams push the limits on engines, restrictor plates, and other methods to get an edge, even when it means breaking the rules. Every year, a handful of teams are penalized for illegally tampering with a car to gain an advantage. But not Joe Gibbs.

"Most people in racing have been of the belief that whatever it took to win races was okay," says Jimmy Makar. "They call it fudging. They call it cheating. They call it lots of things. Joe is of the belief that you do things as hard and as well as you can do them (and) then leave the results to God."

"We make choices all the time," says Gibbs. "And at Joe Gibbs Racing, we say that if we were going to gain from something and it's wrong, we can't do it. And yet, if we would lose by doing something and it's right, we have to do it. We're driven by the fact that we want our principles here to be right in line with the Lord's."

"To walk the talk: I think that's what my dad, if nothing else, he's always done that in my eyes and I think in everyone else's eyes," says son J.D. Gibbs. "He's a man after God's own heart. He's not perfect, and, as usual, the family is the first one to point that out to him. If it's not me or my brother, it's my mom bringing him back down to earth. But he just really wants to do what's right in God's eyes. I think that encompasses so many different traits—loyalty and honesty and hard work—that I was able to witness growing up. It obviously made a big difference in my life."

Joe Gibbs Racing has proven that when excellence becomes a tradition, there is no limit to greatness.

"I would hope that people from the outside would look at this race team and say, 'Hey, those guys are trying to do things the right way; there's something different there about their race team; that's the right way we should be doing things,'" says Joe Gibbs. "(We want) to be a witness through the way we act and the way we race."

CHAPTER TWENTY-TWO

KURT WARNER

His is the Hollywood story; the type that comes along perhaps just once every 50 or so years. It is the kind of story that grabs the attention of media across continents and grabs hearts everywhere. And that is exactly what happened in 1999, when the world discovered Kurt Warner.

In a storybook season, Warner came from football oblivion into the public consciousness and the football record books, leading the St. Louis Rams to the NFL championship. And in the process, he proved that some dreams really do come true. It was the most spectacular and significant rise of any one player during one NFL season in history.

Warner's story is about perseverance, overcoming significant obstacles, and being in the right place at the right time. It s also all about great things happening in the life of a genuinely good human being.

Kurt Warner s odyssey began during the Rams 1999 preseason. The Rams had signed free-agent quarterback, Trent Green, away from the Washington Redskins to lead the Rams in what they felt could be a breakthrough season. But then Green went down with a season-ending knee injury in the Rams next-to-last exhibition game, and the team was suddenly placed in Warner s hands.

No one on the Rams coaching staff knew what to expect. Nor did the players, fans, or anyone else. Few people outside of the Rams organization had even heard of Warner. Worse than a no-name, he was often confused with former Seattle Seahawks running back, Curt Warner, who had retired in 1990. But by the end of the 1999 season, everyone in the sports world had become very familiar with this man and his journey.

Kurt Warner s unlikely path to NFL stardom began in his lone year as a starting quarterback at Division I-AA Northern Iowa, where he sat the bench for four years. When he finally got his shot in 1993, as a fifth-year senior, he led the Panthers to the NCAA Division I-AA semifinals and was named first-team All-Gateway Conference, throwing for 2,747 yards and 17 touchdowns.

That performance earned him a free-agent tryout with the Green Bay Packers in 1994. Warner made it to the Packers' camp for the tryout, but was cut after running just 10 plays in six weeks.

Warner went home to Cedar Falls, Iowa. He moved in with the parents of then-girlfriend, Brenda Carney, and took a job stocking shelves at a 24-hour Hy-Vee supermarket. He continued to prepare for his shot at the NFL, working out and studying football film at his alma mater each day before heading off to work at night. There wasn t much time for sleep.

At the Hy-Vee store, he took home $5.50 an hour while telling co-workers he would someday be playing professional football again.

I think inside they were probably thinking, There s probably no way, I mean this guy s working in a supermarket   how s he ever going to play in the NFL? · says Kurt. They listened to me and humored me at the time, but I m sure deep down nobody really expected me to be able to get to the point where I m at

"I think the Lord put me there for a reason—to test my faith and see where I was so that I would be ready for the situation that I'm in now,"

today, I can t blame them. It s a strange story. If I was looking at things from the outside, I would probably have thought the same things as they did.

Still, local celebrity beyond the checkout counter did come. Out of the blue, the Iowa Barnstormers of the Arena Football League called. At first, Kurt wasn't thrilled about the prospect of playing eight-man football, but he figured it was better than nothing. He struggled initially because he lacked the speed and agility needed for the quick-scoring game. But he adapted and became an Arena ball star, passing for 10,164 yards and 183 touchdowns and leading the Barnstormers to two Arena Bowls in three seasons.

Kurt had all the qualities to be a great quarterback, said Warner s Arena League coach, John Gregory. We knew he had the arm and the intelligence. We just didn t know if he ever would get a chance to show his ability.

I ve always believed in myself, says Warner. I always believed that I had the talent to get to this level and to be successful. . . . I was just waiting for the opportunity. I was waiting for that door to open, to get a chance to prove to everybody that I could do it.

Despite his Arena League success, Kurt couldn t get another look from an NFL team. But then Al Luginbill, the coach of NFL Europe s Amsterdam Admirals, came calling. Warner told Luginbill he d rather keep playing for the Barnstormers for $65,000 a year than go abroad, unless an NFL team signed him and optioned him to Europe for training. A dozen teams told Luginbill no before Charley Armey, the Rams personnel director, decided to take a chance.

Warner then had what he considered a horrible tryout with St. Louis. But during that look-see, he gained two key backersna mely

Armey and assistant coach Mike White, who persuaded the team to sign him. The Rams then sent him to Europe to play for Amsterdam in 1998. It was a smart move. Warner led NFL Europe in passing yardage (2,101) and touchdowns (15), and gained a new level of confidence. And his experiences off the field with the open culture in Amsterdam challenged the conservative quarterback and prepared him to be a leader.

> "Everything that happens to me is just a platform for me to share my faith and to share what I believe. God's bigger than a football game, and He wants to touch people's lives. That's what my goal is, and He gives me the platform."

I think the Lord put me there for a reason to test my faith and see where I was so that I would be ready for the situation that I m in now, says Warner. It gave me an opportunity to strengthen some people that were over there with me. I was able to build some relationships. I think I was able to help mentor some of the guys over there from a Christian standpoint and help keep them where they wanted to be and not fall into the temptations that Amsterdam had surrounding us.

Warner returned to the states in the summer to compete for a spot on the Rams roster. He barely held on to the third-string QB job for St. Louis that fall, nearly being released in favor of journeyman Wil Furrer. While the Rams were going 4□2 in 1998, Warner saw mop-up action in one game, completing just 4 of 11 passes for 39 yards. His future was still very much in doubt.

At the Rams 1999 training camp, Warner moved into the Rams number two quarterback spot to back up Green. When the starter went down, Warner seized the opportunity. Personnel people from around the league watched in amazement as Warner lit up the league s best defenses.

What they saw was a player of average size (6-foot-2, 220 pounds) and speed, but with impressive arm strength, great touch, and the ability to make all the throws—from laser-like deep outs across the field, to feathery-soft corner lobs, to on-the-money long strikes. They saw a man with maturity and leadership intangibles, equipped with pinpoint accuracy, poise under fire, toughness, and an uncanny adeptness for reading defenses very quickly—something that takes rookies three to four years to learn. Playing Arena ball, with its small field and wide-open style, helped Warner become proficient at making quick throws based on even quicker reads. His accuracy was uncanny. When his receivers came out of their breaks, the ball was usually right there.

They also saw a student of the game with a voracious appetite for watching film and an ability to learn. He became known for seeing something once on film or live and never forgetting it. And they saw a quarterback with an unusual feel for the game and an ability to handle pressure.

In the end, 1999 was a year in which Warner generated the second finest statistical single season by a quarterback in NFL history. He completed 65 percent of his passes and threw for 4,353 yards and 41 touchdowns. At the time, only Dan Marino had thrown for more touchdowns in a single season. His passing rating was the third highest all-time. He led the Rams from their 4–12 mark in 1998 to a 13–3 record and a spot in the Super Bowl and was named the NFL's Player of the Year.

At the Super Bowl, Warner eclipsed Joe Montana s 11-year-old passing record by throwing for 414 yards. He completed 24 of 45 passes and tossed two touchdownsi ncluding the game winner with one minute and fifty-four seconds remaining in the contest—and was named the game's Most Valuable Player.

Through it all, he remained unfazed, humble to the core, and ever insistent on keeping the focus off of himself.

My faith is the most important thing, says Warner. Everything that happens to me is just a platform for me to share my faith and to share what I believe. God s bigger than a football game, and He wants to touch people s lives. That s what my goal is, and He gives me the platform.

Kurt s the most grounded person you ll ever meet, says former teammate Todd Lyght.

That grounding has shown throughout his career, which has seen him have success with the New York Giants and Arizona Cardinals since leaving St. Louis and seen him battle through numerous injuries. Still, he has been one of the most prolific NFL quarterbacks for over a decade. The person who is most unfazed by his accomplishments is Warner himself.

I fell through the cracks just because of the fact that nobody saw me play, says Warner. I only played one year in college and it was at a small schoola nd I played well that one year, but it s hard to put a lot of stock in just one year. It s hard to give a guy that hasn t played very much a great opportunity. To me, it was more that nobody ever saw me play and could really gauge what kind of quarterback I was because they weren t looking in the right places.

Kurt Warner is. . .an example of what we all like to believe in on and off the field," said former Rams' coach Dick Vermiel. "He is an example of persistence and believing in himself and a deep faith. He was willing to work and play a subordinate role until he got his opportunity. What else can you write? He is a book; he is a movie, the guy.

The biggest thing I ve learned is that there is a plan for me, says Warner. We don t always know what that plan is going to be, or how we re going to get therebut I ve learned a lot along the way. I ve learned about perseverance. I ve learned about being humble; being able to enjoy everything that I ve gotten. I wouldn t change anything from the way it has turned out. I ve become a better player and a better person throughout the experiences I ve had. I wouldn t change anything. This is as good a script as I could have ever written. ■

ABOUT THE AUTHOR

STEVE RIACH

Steve Riach is a principal and founder of SER Media, a Dallas-based media company. He is an award-winning producer, writer, and director of numerous television, film, documentary, and video projects and is one of the nation s foremost creators of virtuous and positive-themed sports content. Steve's programs have been seen on ESPN, FOX Sports, NBC, and a variety of broadcast and cable television outlets. He is also the principal mind behind the creative vision for the *Heart of a Champion®* brand. His start in sports media came as an on-air personality, hosting national television and radio programming.

A prolific writer, Steve has authored best-selling *Amazing But True Sports Stories* as well as *Passion for the Game, Above the Rim, The Drive to Win, Inspire a Dream, It s How You Play the Game, Life Lessons from Auto Racing, Life Lessons from Golf, Life Lessons from Baseball, Heart of a Champion: Profiles in Character,* and *Amazing Athletes, Amazing Moments, Par for the Course,* and *Girl Power.*

Steve is the co-founder of the *Heart of a Champion® Foundation*, a nonprofit organization devoted to producing materials designed to instill character and ethics in youth. Steve is creator and author of the foundation s innovative **Heart of a Champion®** *Character Development Program*, a leading tool for the character education of students in schools, after school outlets, and juvenile justice programs across America.

Schools in 15 states use Steve s **Heart of a Champion®** educational curriculum, and Fortune 500 companies have employed his corporate training program. Both have produced dramatic, measurable results in lives and bottom-lines.

Steve is also a former college baseball player and a cancer survivor. He speaks to youth organizations, corporations, nonprofits, educational conferences, churches, and sports organizations.

A native of southern California, Steve and his family now make their home in Colleyville, Texas.

ABOUT THE PHOTOGRAPHER

TOM DIPACE

Tom s experience as a professional sports photographer is unsurpassed. Published in notable publications such as *Time, Newsweek, ESPN Magazine, Sports Illustrated, Sports Illustrated for Kids,* and *USA Today,* he is considered one of the top sports photographers in America. His commercial clients include Rawlings Sporting Goods, Wheaties, EA Sports, and 2KSports.

Tom's award-winning work reflects his passion, which is especially evident in his celebrity sports work. His photography is an extension of his personalitya   true expression of art.

HEART OF A CHAMPION

The Heart of a Champion® Foundation is an independent, national nonprofit organization utilizing the platform of sports to build and reinforce character and virtue in young people. Blending the message and the messenger, the Heart of a Champion® Foundation s winning formula teaches and models character education at the grassroots level to mold better citizens and develop the heart of a champion in youth.

The Heart of a Champion® school program is a unique, in-class character education program that teaches positive character values and traits through video, audio, and written vignettes featuring popular and respected athletes and other individuals. It teaches virtues through sight and sound stories of positive role models, attracts the attention of learners, and arouses their interest, raising questions that lead to discussions and reflections about the implementation of those virtues into the daily life process. These stories demonstrate values such as honesty, perseverance, courage, commitment, discipline, integrity, and fairness and encourage students to recognize and follow their examples. The Heart of a Champion® program also includes student, teacher, and parent enrichment materials to reinforce the positive character traits that are taught and discussed. The Heart of a Champion® Foundation believes that training young people in character and virtue can help build the champions of tomorrow through stories of the heroes of today.

The Heart of a Champion® Corporate Learning program is a unique ethics training program that addresses root-cause issues and is proven to create measurable attitudinal and behavioral change and performance enhancement and to produce bottomline results.

For more information on all of the Heart of a Champion® programs, visit the Web sites at www.heartofachampion.org and www.hoctraining.com, or call (817) 427-4621.

Heart of a Champion is a registered trademark under which virtuous sports products and programs are created and distributed, including award-winning videos, television and radio programs, films and books.